W0081900

REALLY
RICH

REALLY RICH

The Ten
Future-Proof Behaviors
That Create Wealth

NICHOLAS CROWN

hachette
BOOKS

New York

Copyright © 2025 by Nicholas Crown
Cover design and illustration by YY Liak
Cover copyright © 2025 by Hachette Book Group, Inc.

Hachette Book Group supports the right to free expression and the value of copyright. The purpose of copyright is to encourage writers and artists to produce the creative works that enrich our culture.

The scanning, uploading, and distribution of this book without permission is a theft of the author's intellectual property. If you would like permission to use material from the book (other than for review purposes), please contact Permissions@hbgusa.com. Thank you for your support of the author's rights.

Hachette Go, an imprint of Hachette Books
Hachette Book Group
1290 Avenue of the Americas
New York, NY 10104
HachetteGo.com
Facebook.com/HachetteGo
Instagram.com/HachetteGo

First Edition: January 2025

Published by Hachette Go, an imprint of Hachette Book Group, Inc. The Hachette Go name and logo are trademarks of the Hachette Book Group.

The publisher is not responsible for websites (or their content) that are not owned by the publisher.

The Hachette Speakers Bureau provides a wide range of authors for speaking events. To find out more, go to hachettespeakersbureau.com or email HachetteSpeakers@hbgusa.com.

Hachette Go books may be purchased in bulk for business, educational, or promotional use. For information, please contact your local bookseller or email the Hachette Book Group Special Markets Department at Special.Markets@hbgusa.com.

Print book interior design by Amy Quinn

Library of Congress Cataloging-in-Publication Data

Name: Crown, Nicholas, author.
Title: Really rich: the ten future-proof behaviors that create wealth / Nicholas Crown.
Description: First edition. | New York, NY: Hachette Go, 2025. | Includes bibliographical references and index.
Identifiers: LCCN 2024023708 | ISBN 9780306834257 (trade paperback) | ISBN 9780306834264 (ebook)
Subjects: LCSH: Wealth. | Rich people—Conduct of life. | Success in business.
Classification: LCC HC79.W4 C76 2025 | DDC 305.5/234—dc23/eng/20240712
LC record available at https://lccn.loc.gov/2024023708

ISBNs: 978-0-306-83425-7 (trade paperback), 978-0306834264 (ebook)

Printed in the United States of America

LSC-C

Printing 1, 2024

To the viewers, listeners, likers, and commentors who encouraged me to keep going

Contents

Contents

Introduction

THE TEN FUTURE-PROOF BEHAVIORS
THAT CREATE WEALTH

THE TWO MES

I DID EVERYTHING THEY TOLD ME TO DO—COMB MY HAIR, SCORE high on the SAT, fight my way into a good school, graduate with honors, get a job on Wall Street, work hard and ignore everything else—every whimper or complaint that might pathetically emerge on my trail to victory—until I'm rich, so very rich, and then, and only then, can I tell everyone to screw off. That was the deal, do *this* and get *that*: suffer a bit just to get what I'm really after. It was an unquestionable recipe. Doing the opposite would certainly prove ruinous.

Some might call this conventional wisdom. Others might call it listening to "Mom and Dad," and that's whether you were born in Bangalore or Beacon Hill. And perhaps yours isn't even about Wall Street—maybe it's law or medicine or whatever's still hot in your neck of the woods. I did all this slavishly: I was a master of doing everything by the book, a golden boy, yet, in return for my efforts, one day everything went perfectly wrong.

In 2010, at twenty-three years of age I was a bond trader in New York, living the culmination of a childhood of academic strife, when

I noticed that all five of my computer screens were blinking—red, red, red. Not good. Naturally, for a closer look, I took my heels off the desk, which is where they had been poised as I showed off for an intern shadowing me that day. What I saw didn't seem possible—the market couldn't have moved that much. Those around me one by one stood up and put their hands to their heads in disbelief. Someone shouted, "It's all over!" *All* meaning life itself—the end of the world. I realized that things were about to go very wrong for me.

When you're a trader, you lust for all things green—hundred-dollar bills, upticks, Viper Green Porsches—but you despise red. Red means you're losing. Even when you don't have a position on the amount of security, asset, or property you're trading, you mourn the downticks and cheer the ups. You say a prayer for the poor joker down the row from you who has to tell his wife they're not going to the Hamptons again this summer. Until this moment, I had never seen so much money being lost in my entire life.

And it was all from my account.

I had just shorted several hundred million dollars of bond futures into the most bull-crazy market I had ever seen. In other words: I was losing hundreds of thousands of dollars every second. Of course, I was witnessing what would later become known as the 2010 Flash Crash, a global stock market crash and bond market rally (bonds "crash up" as individuals flee from risky things like stocks to the government bond safe haven). My limit orders were triggered by the enormous movement in bond prices. I was naked, not hedged, short, and in deep trouble.

My first inclination was to reach for the wastebasket under my desk to vomit. But, as if they were presented on a silver platter from the universe, I instead saw plainly that I had two options, and I had to decide immediately:

- End life as I know it
- Trade out of it

I decided to trade out of it.

And trade out of it I did—buying spreads at God-awful prices and flipping them back at even more absurd prices to anyone who would take them. As I moved my mouse around the screen in an attempt to save my life, I asked myself a pressing question: Why was I was even here in the first place? Why hadn't I stuck with advertising, one of my first internships, where I would be fretting over the perfect tagline for a soft drink campaign rather than facing being questioned in a court of law, potentially, for unsound risk parameters or being labeled the next "rogue trader"? I thought I was here to make money and escape my parents' house.

By the time I returned my position to flat, my shirt was soaked through with sweat, and the intern standing next to me looked like he had seen a ghost. He kept mouthing, "What happened? What happened?" Several moments ago I was down millions of dollars. Now? Only thirty grand, or, as we high-risk traders call it, "scratch" or, better yet, a "rounding error." I had survived somehow.

The boss "upstairs" (off of the trading floor) came down to address the commotion. "Holy shit," he stammered, "is everything okay? Are you hedged?" I pretended to look confused and shrugged, "Yeah, of course." When I walked into my apartment that night, I sat on a chair in my entryway to unlace my shoes. I woke up right there in my clothes the next morning.

We used to toss around a joke in the elevator on the way up to the office: "Living the dream!" we'd exclaim sarcastically, tacitly understanding we were inmates in an Alcatraz of our own design. Most of us had spent our entire childhood praying we'd end up here.

My parents separated when I was seven years old. They broke the news to my brother and me in a back booth at a cheap Mexican restaurant in the low-income suburb of East Orange, New Jersey. After the divorce, I strived to be the perfect son. Attention from a parent in a chaotic divorced household, as approximately 50 percent of the population are well aware, is like gold bullion. I imagined myself as something of an adolescent Renaissance intellectual—painting, playing guitar, reading a book a week. That is, before I learned about money. And money, as it usually does, changed things.

After high school, I was accepted into Cornell University, which was part of my plan all along. I'd salivated over the prestige of a fancy diploma and the income that would come along with it upon graduation for as long as I could remember.

I loved it all, especially dragging a pony keg through the snow to save the day for a last-minute impromptu party—*Holy shit, more beer!* I was the social chair of my fraternity, wielding a budget in the deca-thousands monthly, responsible for more than a few outrageous parties.

In retrospect, though, I learned very little of practical value at Cornell. I remember the parties and stunts (calculating whether I could indeed jump from the balcony and land on the couch below), but I can't recall a single class lesson that stood out—except the finance classes, which seemed like a pathetic facsimile of the real thing. Even I knew a real financier wouldn't waste his precious time teaching a bunch of hungover slobs in a lecture hall. And this is sad, because I didn't miss a single class like some of my more cavalier classmates, several of whom ended up not walking with me during graduation. I sat through every single one.

My dream at the time was to become rich—though I had little idea what that meant, short of imagining that more money would bring more independence and freedom—and so I dropped any thoughts of an artistic pursuit and majored instead in Applied Economics (as opposed to "unapplied economics," I suppose), the quackery of pure academia with supply and demand curves on graph paper.

Miraculously, I scored an interview with a decent-sized bank straightaway (one that ended up among the largest after Lehman Brothers fell) with an interviewer who, with a tattered shirt and two-day old stubble, looked like he should have been committed to an insane asylum. After a minor shouting match (social norms are viewed merely as time-wasters for old traders), I passed the test and thus began my career in the belly of Wall Street, on the trading floor, trading repurchase agreements, or "repos" (otherwise known to insiders as the "asshole of the bond market"), with a crew of outcast misfits who had the ability to survive the mental onslaught of working day in and day out in the markets, which opened at the ungodly hour of 4:30 a.m. in New York.

It didn't take long to realize that the Wall Street I was in was nothing like the Wall Street portrayed by Hollywood. Suits were stained from the late nights and everyone's shirts were ripped at the elbows from grinding into their desk during the trading day. One out of every fifty heads was making real money. The rest, barely hanging on, were generally overleveraged penny-pinchers who lived miserable lives in cheaper suburbs with a two-hour commute to Manhattan each way. They never saw their kids. They were the living dead.

I joined an experimental group called Futures RV (Relative Value) around the corner from my first desk. And by *joined*, I mean I begged my way into the desk. I think the managing director who ran the thing saw pure desperation. And here, *desperation* usually means opportunity.

Although we were still tech dinosaurs compared to the folks in Silicon Valley, we operated far more like a software company that happened to be run by traders. A Guatemalan colleague of mine suggested he would carve up with a knife anyone who interrupted him during the trading day. He came close to it once. In this environment, I made a name for myself fast by understanding the complex technology and the micro-opportunities of trading spreads. My new MD, let's call him Bob, caught on. Bringing me on had been a good trade.

In a few months, Bob jumped ship to another well-known investment bank, and I was his first phone call, in part because I knew spread-trading technology inside and out—these are computer-based trading systems with the ability to shift many millions of dollars at the press of a button. The best part was I could do this in a way that no one noticed by slicing huge trades into tiny slices that barely made a ripple. Bob figured, as expensive as I was— and, by then, I was expensive—hiring me would be like a cheap call option, to the extent one pays a fixed premium for unlimited upside.

I was given a "blank check" deal, as they're known in the business, and made up a bonus number that I thought simply couldn't be possible to attain. Also, part of the deal was that I'd be ushered in with the hallowed status of Director at this bank, which was unheard of because I was by now just entering my late twenties. They bit. When the signing bonus hit my account, I rented a new one-bedroom apartment in a famed high-rise on Park Avenue where the guitarist Eric Clapton used to live and bought a leather couch from Design Within Reach.

SEVERAL MONTHS INTO THE ROLE, MY NEW EMPLOYER SAW ME AS someone with a lot still to learn in the leadership department, and they insisted I attend a "Rising Stars" corporate conference to hone my skills. Banks, and often also large law and marketing firms, are notorious for sponsoring such large conferences for their administrative staff and younger employees to motivate them at their desk jobs or train them to effectively work together. One part cheap vacation in a bland corporate hotel and two parts voyeuristically spying to see who drinks too much at the open bar. I couldn't imagine a worse hell on earth.

Low-level employees often view these as days off, away from their work grind—an opportunity to stay overnight at a decent hotel, eat for free, and drink their asses off. For traders, it was a risky venture that put your book, your business, at risk; created missed opportunities to make money; and compelled you to hang out with people who have no clue what you do all day long but revere you in a slightly creepy way, like an A-list celebrity.

When I was told about one particular conference, I chuckled: "Yeah, right!" But that was met with, "I wasn't asking," an insinuation that I'd be canned if I didn't attend the event.

And so I dragged myself up to a conference center in Stamford, Connecticut, in a custom-made charcoal suit and black monk straps and registered the results of my Myers-Briggs analysis, a psychological assessment designed to measure and categorize different personality types. Supposedly, the personality assessment would be used to ensure I "got the most" out of the weekend. I smelled conspiracy.

The entire conference was emceed by a hyperexcitable Australian guy, some sort of professional motivator I suppose, who gathered everyone together and asked us to stand up according to personality type. I don't recall where I scored on that assessment, but out of thousands of test-takers I was the only one who stood for the particular trait that the Aussie barked out last. The entire auditorium turned to look at me, like: "Who the hell is this guy? What a freak!"

I wasn't interested in the presentations, I didn't attend the happy hours, and I certainly didn't require further motivation: what I was mostly doing was worrying about my book and how it was performing in my absence. On the second day, they had us in business formal attire searching around for clues in a grass field behind the hotel in some sick attempt at a scavenger hunt dressed up as a "business experiment." A violent death would have been welcomed with open arms by me at this point.

By the end of the conference I had come to a scary and unexpected insight: I didn't belong here in this freakish world of mediocre automatons. I felt as though I was sold some cheap trick in exchange for my youth and dignity. What did I want to do? For sure, I wanted to be wealthy, I knew that. But I no longer wanted to be a salaried worker, no matter how high that salary was. What was I good at? That was a very interesting question, and one that was harder to answer. People generally liked me, and I was good at making them laugh. I enjoyed "performing" for friends, telling stories and cutting up, and certainly I enjoyed the attention. I was definitely good at my job, but I hated it—so those skills didn't make the list. There was one other thing, though: I was a pretty good guitarist, songwriter, and singer, and I loved listening to the blues, especially contemporary blues bands like the Black Keys. For these last few moments, my life looked pretty good on paper.

During my Leadership Exit Interview, my facilitator asked, "So, Nick, what did you think about the weekend? I think this group grew on you since you walked in if I had to guess." They had all referred to me as an "asshole" during our first-impressions "Honesty Experiment." I stated, "I'm quitting the first moment I get when I'm back on my desk tomorrow." My facilitator simply raised her eyebrows and wrote something in her notebook.

I walked into work the next day ready to pull out of my vein the bank-salary IV that was pumping thousands of dollars into my system every two weeks. Now, walking away from a job like this in your twenties, after a relatively meteoric rise, means there's no coming back—once I was out, I was out. On Wall Street, once you leave, you're never allowed back. I'd be crossing the proverbial Rubicon and burning the goddamn boats.

When I tapped Bob, my MD, on the shoulder and said I wanted to talk (code for "quit" on the Street), he narrowed his eyes and asked, "Are you high?"

People thought I had lost my mind. And, to be fair, I didn't really have a plan going forward; I just knew I couldn't stick around and grow old and bitter on a trading floor. Many I once thought of as friends were whispering that I was a loser, a quitter, and probably a chump. Leaving the Street at the top of your game usually means you had a crack-up; no one would willingly forfeit millions of dollars like that.

My parents were apoplectic—my father especially so, telling me over veal Milanese in an Upper East Side Italian joint to take a long, hard look at what I had just done. What a waste of an education, he said, reminding me I was the first in the family to attend an Ivy League school and earn a job at a top bank. Unwrapping a sleeve of breadsticks, I started to wonder if I had made a grave mistake.

After kicking around Europe for more than a year, drinking cheap wine and recording some early music that maybe ten people listened to, I returned home to join some old friends on a road trip down South. After all, I didn't have anything better to do. One of our stops was New Orleans. New Orleans blues, of course, is a genre all its own, a big, funky sound that incorporates elements of jazz, rhythm and blues, traditional African rhythms, gospel music, ragtime, and the brass band tradition of New Orleans.

The madness and poverty and celebration of the town transfixed me. A haunted hospital, abandoned since Hurricane Katrina, still hung over the city. I thought: I'm going to move here.

As an ex-trader, a former institutional banker, that's ridiculous. New Orleans was a place to tell a tall tale of how you got your Rolex stolen during a bachelor party, not a place to live. But the more I thought about it, the more I yearned to try. The idea took hold and wouldn't let go: Yeah, I can do this, and, not only that, I think I can be good enough to get rich from it.

One morning, after an all-nighter and a few hours of sleep in a creepy hotel a block from Bourbon Street, I informed my road-trip friends. "Guys," I said, "I'm not coming back with you. You're going to leave me here." When they realized I wasn't joking, they reluctantly agreed. On the way out, I swear the doorman traveled through a wall to hand me my luggage. These are the kinds of things that become commonplace in New Orleans.

Soon enough, thanks to Craigslist, I found a place to stay and put together a band. We did some covers, I wrote all of our new material, and we gradually made a name for ourselves in town, performing somewhere almost every night. At our peak about a year later, we won a local radio contest for "Best New Band," which resulted in a gig at the New Orleans House of Blues, recording opportunities, and discussions with agents and record producers. As it turns out, a Grammy-winning producer, Dave Fortman, who broke the platinum act Evanescence, caught one of our shows and, at no cost, helped put out our first record.

The band was composed of me and an assortment of local fuck-ups with hearts of gold. I loved them dearly. After a heavy bout of drinking, my bass player allowed me to sleep in his closet for a day because we'd both determined I would feel safe in there. To be honest, it was actually pretty cozy.

It was that kind of relationship.

I carried the entire venture for more than two years—a noble but lavish effort that drained my bank account. By the time it became apparent that our hopes for a record deal were going nowhere, I was broke. As in, from millions down to a few thousand bucks. And, of course, when the money stopped flowing, the band fell apart. They didn't take too well to me running a band like it was a trading desk—with nonstop work and cutthroat seriousness. I'd pace around and examine areas of the musical track and request obscure changes that I'll swear by to this day. One time, I had the recording engineer locate a glockenspiel, something you've maybe seen in a high school band room, for a fifteen-second break in a track. It wasn't for everyone.

After the heights of earning I had enjoyed on Wall Street and three years of traveling and trying to make it as a musician, I was screwed. I couldn't even pay my next month's rent, which was all of twelve hundred bucks—a paltry sum that looked more like my dry cleaning bill when I'd lived on Park Avenue a few years before. I had chased what I believed was my dream, I tried everything to make it work, but I had failed. It was excruciating to admit this to myself. This was it.

DESPERATE, I WAS REDUCED TO CALLING AN OLD FRIEND FROM MY New York days who designed men's clothing for a small chain of stores with an outpost in New Orleans. Assuming I was peddling some kind of start-up or financial advisory package, she laughed and said, "You don't know shit about fashion. What are you trying to sell them? *Accounting* software?" I explained that I needed a job, any job, before my landlord kicked me out, and she soberly replied, "Okay, sure, let me make a call."

She recommended me as a sales clerk at the store, and after a twenty-minute coffee with a store manager who was about five years younger than me, there I was in New Orleans fetching shirts and shoes for customers to try on. Ironically, from my days of getting bespoke suits cut every other week at my tailor in the Flatiron District of Manhattan, I knew a ton about menswear—at least from a rich customer's perspective. Being on the other end of the transaction was supremely humbling, to say the least. Often, I'd strike up conversation with a customer, trying to connect with them around a business or finance topic, only for them to smile and nod and gesture for me to pull a half size larger from the stockroom. Would you have listened to me either?

During my fifteen-minute breaks, I would hide out in the back, feverishly trying to figure out what went wrong and what the hell I would do next. My work colleagues used the proceeds from their efforts at the store to get blind drunk nightly in a string of local bars a stone's throw from the storefront. Feeling high and mighty was useless, because if all those around you are drunks and losers, then guess what? You are too. This realization sizzled the back of my neck. I had destroyed my entire life.

I couldn't go back to Wall Street—that unforgiving culture wouldn't take me back. Music was also now a dead end. Lord knows, I wasn't gunning for store manager at the men's shop, where my salary would skyrocket to all of eighteen dollars an hour, four dollars more than I was making on the store's showroom.

Still, my basic desire hadn't changed. I needed money, and I wanted to be rich. But not salary rich, *really rich*. I just needed to spot an opportunity. At the present moment, looking around, it was clear there was zero opportunity for me at the store, or in New Orleans, for that matter.

But I did have a laptop.

From the breakroom, I scanned online gig listings, places where freelancers could score more than twenty dollars an hour doing creative projects like graphic design or even fractional business consulting. I saw there was a huge need for résumé writing—with tons of requests and few freelancers jumping in to fill the need. I could always write, and I'd even harbored a sick fascination for formatting my papers in school. And at one time I had been the one *reviewing* the résumés.

I figured if I took a few cheap gigs and built up a portfolio, I could raise my prices and focus on working only with executives—what I had once been a lifetime ago. From the breakroom, I wrote my first résumé. It turns out, I was good at it, and the market indeed was robust—within four months, I was making over $10,000 a month. So, I did what any young guy with a little money in his pocket would do.

I moved to Miami.

In Miami, I linked up with an old friend from New York, a good-natured trust-funder from the Upper West Side who, over a spicy tuna roll, said he had someone I had to meet. He introduced me to Ed.

Ed was running a massively successful digital consulting business. He wasn't just making money, he was having fun. He was often seen peeling out of the entrance of his luxury condo building in a twelve-cylinder Aston Martin coupe. His place had $100K of modern furniture in it—the stuff you see in showrooms that makes young, urban males salivate. I wanted all that—it was far more than my buddies on Wall Street ever had. So I made myself useful to Ed, providing humor and commentary where needed during a few social events. Lord knows, I didn't have enough cash to roll with him. Mostly, I listened, which is a priceless commodity on the plastic shores of Miami Beach.

He generously invited me to, essentially, trail him, and he taught me the basics of the digital agency business. My goal was to earn $100,000 per month, a nice round number, something Ed had ticked off his list a few years ago. Doing this would take single-minded focus, to the exclusion of virtually everything else, including any form of social life. Within six months, I generated more than ten clients, at a $10,000 per month retainer each, and hit my earnings goal. Within eighteen months, my bank account was back to where it was before I set off on my music adventure. Suddenly, I was rich again.

But there was one big problem.

I didn't *feel* rich.

My agency clients treated me worse than the shoppers who made me fetch shoes in New Orleans.

I was not free by any means—having a beer with dinner or dinner out on the town was out of the question lest I curb any of the mental clarity necessary for withstanding another day of barraging questions. I was living like a monk.

Neither was I free to enjoy all the other aspects of life that I also wanted besides wealth. I wanted good health. I wanted time to go to the gym every day. I wanted to see friends. I wanted time for a satisfying love life. It turned out that it wasn't nearly enough for me to earn $100,000 per month to the exclusion of everything else. It wasn't worth it to be owned and used, essentially, like a donkey— whether I was ridden by my investment bank bosses or my digital consultancy clients.

And this is when my life took an unexpected turn.

I HAD BEEN AWARE OF SOCIAL MEDIA, OF COURSE, BUT I WAS THE sort of guy who might post once in a while on Facebook or Instagram—*Hi everyone, I'm in Poland today! Why the fuck am I in Poland?* I'd post a photo of food and get fifteen likes, two of which were from my parents. Not exactly influencer material.

What I did not realize, at all, was what I will refer to throughout this work as the *leverage* of social media. More importantly, and the reason why I'm writing this book, is that I did not realize until the moment I stepped away from my successful consultancy that there's a very, very big difference—think in terms of an abyss—between being rich and being *really rich*.

It came to me in a flash: Ed was *really rich*. Whereas I couldn't stand my digital agency business, Ed not only thrived in his but also had crafted a lifestyle perfectly suited to him, one in which he loved what he did, was very wealthy, and had time to pursue his many other interests. What worked for Ed didn't work for me. Just as I'm sure there are a few lunatics who enjoy getting onto the trading floor at 4:30 a.m. as much as I abhor it.

Becoming Really Rich, in a nutshell, means establishing a thing—a product, a service, an artistic endeavor—that you love, that you're uniquely good at, and that, *most importantly*, the market responds to. This means other people have to want what you have to offer; otherwise, you're at best a hobbyist, at worst an ego-driven jackass pushing unwanted things onto the market. I damn sure didn't want to be "that guy" in the band everyone felt sorry for, middling about until I turned forty.

I wasn't Really Rich on Wall Street or with my digital consultancy because neither engaged me or brought out my best self. I had only half the equation figured out. More to the point, I wasn't Really Rich as a blues musician—in fact, I was poor—because the market did not value what I was producing. We never sold more than a few dozen concert tickets and never made it to the cover of *Rolling Stone*, which was my dream at the time.

The key to becoming Really Rich, as will become apparent in this work, is to discover what you love and what you're good at and continue to iterate until the market responds by showering you with wealth and a status bump—the two historic elements by which people in any given market respond to the value that you create and offer.

Although my arrival on social media was methodical, what happened next was pure iteration. I had listened to a short podcast with Naval Ravikant, the founder of AngelList, who explained that social media was a brand-new form of leverage in society that was both permissionless (videos go viral algorithmically when more people engage with them, not via a single gatekeeper) and scalable (copies of your videos are shown on everyone's phone, free to the creator to disseminate). While floating around in my buddy's rooftop swimming pool, I thought very clearly, *I can do this.*

I made a thirty-day bet with myself: make one TikTok video a day for thirty days, without telling a soul, and see what happens. If it doesn't work out, no one will know; if it works out, everyone will know, and I'll be an online celebrity. This is the definition, as I'd later learn to call it, of testing and iteration.

So after a few half-baked TikTok posts about digital nomading and digital marketing—well-worn social media paths—I came up with an idea to do what I'm good at: performing. I created two characters—the Rich Guy and Really Rich Guy—and began to explore different scenarios to illustrate the two lifestyles. I simply plopped both characters in a steakhouse setting and let them talk to the waiter. One was out to waste your time and position himself as a discerning diner; the other simply wanted to be left alone to eat in peace. Of course, both characters were me. I had lived the cranky, self-important life on Wall Street as Rich Guy, but began to see another way of doing business as I crashed, burned, and started over again, a more open-minded way with a long-term viewpoint.

The video gained millions of views overnight: the market not only liked what I was creating but also liked it in a big way. And when you've iterated and reiterated until something works, well, you just keep slamming that button until the market has had enough.

Within days, the themes I explored across all the major social media channels, primarily TikTok and YouTube, grew more serious in their intent. People were hungry to understand and be entertained by the differences between a rich, arrogant, usually salaryman lifestyle and a really rich, unpretentious, typically entrepreneurial one: Question your own boundaries. Apply kindness in all interactions. Consider your quality of life. Recognize that time, not money, is your greatest asset. I put the characters in challenges to show how each one would escape—one would run through walls, one would find a key and stroll out the front door.

You see, when you're Really Rich, the future—whether in artificial intelligence or in other innovative fields to come—only grows richer for everyone. Getting the market to respond, of course, depends on your ability to iterate and reiterate your idea, product, or service, and it also crucially is a function of time. The most amazing part is, as long as you're in the market iterating on something you enjoy, you'll hit gold eventually. This was a far cry from the rapid, bloodthirsty competition I once called home on Wall Street. Finally, the light bulb went on for me.

WHAT'S IN IT FOR YOU

Over the course of developing Rich vs. Really Rich scenarios, I synthesized a system for how to actually become Really Rich. A system that didn't just work for me but that would work for anyone: visionary start-up founder to mom-and-pop business owner. By producing skit after skit, and picking apart their elements like it was a science project, I ultimately forged what I present in this book: the underlying behaviors that every person can utilize to become Really Rich. You will learn how to make these behaviors your own and effectively wield them to cut your own path forward.

As children, we're drilled with a mix of common sense and downright lies about the way the world works. I hope to provide sound reasoning behind the "whys" and dispel the misinformation that keeps many, including myself, confused and punching below their weight for many years. This isn't some gooey message from an overly doting mother who's terrified of you crossing the street. We will redefine common words—*value, luck, kindness,* and *wealth* among them—with new meanings. In fact, this new vocabulary will soon allow you to spot patterns all around you.

When traders uncover profitable strategies, they begin a process of "backtesting" to see how profitable the strategy would have been at various points throughout history. Would I have made money during the 2008 crash? You simply run the data through your algorithm. Similarly, I've backtested these Really Rich principles using the stories of friends and Gilded Age titans alike, and they've been proven true every time. If you pick me up and drop me in Mesopotamia, they'd still apply. After all, what good is a system that wanes in usefulness as we move forward (or backward) in time and innovation? Things certainly will be different in the future than they are today—we want a model for value creation that's timeless. In this book, you're going to get the goods.

Shockingly, I've found that these behaviors are also *costless* to add to your own life and require little to no education. They leverage what you already know and care about, which inherently makes you far more informed on the topic than I am. For example, offers to "pay your way" into a new business venture would fail compared to a strategy of taking the time to truly understand what the market wants in the first place. After reading this book, and internalizing the Really Rich behaviors, you will not be disadvantaged compared to any of the bravest, best-capitalized entrepreneurs.

Further, if implemented correctly, the behaviors will improve all aspects of your life: relationships, money, and connection to your work. There's no corner-cutting or settling in the land of the Really Rich. And some of the work will be hard.

You'll soon learn that when you create something good, the world can't help but reward you. In fact, the rewards are so connected to what you've provided, you couldn't stop them from coming even if you tried, like a celebrity escaping the paparazzi. You get paid whether you like it or not.

I've expressed here, as concisely as I can, the most valuable thing I can offer: a comprehensive understanding of the way people work and reward each other. Although the principles presented here are simple, they are also new and fresh, and certain passages will require a reread. Once you understand each area, you'll see how each behavior fits together and supports the others like a lattice. Once you put it into motion, you'll see the world through an entirely new lens that makes it less confusing, frustrating, and cold than it was before.

At its heart, the key to living a Really Rich lifestyle lies in iterating and reiterating your value-creative ideas until the market responds with profits and positive status. And anyone can do this with many of their own innate gifts, even if those gifts have sat dormant while the person works a job they hate in a town they wish they could escape. Whether you believe it right now or not, you have something we (humankind) want.

From my time on Wall Street, I learned firsthand that competitiveness—or "rich" behavior—can only take you so far in terms of experience and wealth. Rather, open-mindedness and creativity, or Really Rich behaviors, are truly unbounded. Here, we don't wage war against our competitors or the guy who got the promotion; rather, we play our own true game against ourselves, following our passions and testing them in the marketplace for a nibble.

You'll learn from local heroes, celebrities, titans of industry, lotto winners, and the guy who owns the beloved Italian restaurant on my block in Chicago, which is the city I now call home. All have some critical insights that prove the validity of the Really Rich model. Soon, you'll realize why you can learn something from everyone—no matter where they are in life.

There are many roads to walk to amass wealth and notoriety, but Really Rich behavior allows you to do so creatively and proudly, without guilt, and in a way that makes the world a more interesting place to live.

Your behaviors will include the following:

- *Create value.* Grow rich by making someone else's life easier.
- *Give the market what it wants.* The market, not you, decides what's valuable.
- *Iterate forever.* Tinker and reinvent until someone starts clapping.
- *Understand and appreciate that time is priceless.*

- *Optimize for quality of life, not a dollar amount.*
- *Exude kindness as an accelerant to wealth.*
- *Get humble to cross the boundary between Rich and Really Rich.*
- *Abandon rudeness.*
- *Ignore status because it impedes growth.*
- *Lean on creativity to become future-proof.*

This isn't some clickbait-worthy Top Ten list designed to stop you in your tracks. The Really Rich system is exhaustive, researched, and honed. There is no fat to trim. Further, you won't need to search beyond this framework: it's complete and self-contained. Anything else is sheer subject-matter information that you'll need in order to pursue your chosen craft.

Don't believe me?

Good.

I intend to shatter your worldview one page at a time.

Allow me to get technical for a moment. There may be a lot of criticism about social media and the unfolding artificial intelligence boom, but the truth is that the world is shifting from a mass-market economy to an economy that is customized, specialized, and economically boundless. It is a shift, essentially, from a zero-sum game to one that is non-zero-sum. In a non-zero-sum game, it's possible for all players to win equally as big. In fact, another person's wins end up further propelling your own success. When you win, so do I.

And although every one of the Really Rich behaviors relies on leveraging technology to some extent, each of us will take a separate path. Your map is different from mine, because we're different people, with different dreams, different visions, and different skill sets.

Those of us, however, who find the courage to apply these behaviors to our entrepreneurial life and stick with them will inevitably become Really Rich. This is the world we live in. This book shows you how it all works.

CHAPTER 1

The World Is Not Zero-Sum

MICHAEL JORDAN IS ARGUABLY THE BEST BASKETBALL PLAYER in history. Perhaps you, like me, consider him to be the greatest overall athlete of all time. On the court, Jordan played a clear, zero-sum game, with winners (usually him) and losers (usually someone else)—with his six NBA championships, he was notorious for his capacity to win, sometimes in crushing fashion. You didn't want to go head-to-head with Jordan in a pinch on the court.

However, off the court, far from the cheering Chicago Bulls fans, Jordan elevated the sport of basketball and the earnings potential of all players for eternity. Yes, even for the Cavs and Pistons. I'd go as far as to say that he elevated professional sports in general. He did this largely by popularizing his sport, helping it become a global phenomenon—today's players, many of them far less talented than Jordan, have the ability to earn far more than Jordan had. This financial pandemonium had the side effect of spreading into other popular sports, like football and baseball, and even tennis and golf. Would there really be a Tiger Woods without the precedent of Jordan?

As a rookie, in the 1984–1985 season, Jordan earned close to the league minimum—a total of $550,000 or about $1.6 million in today's dollars. By 1997–1998, his annual salary was $33 million—the highest ever at the time. Several of today's NBA stars have surpassed even that figure, with Steph Curry in 2021–2022 earning more than $45 million, which is awfully close to Jordan after accounting for inflation. In fact, some fifteen players have been paid more than $40 million since Jordan hung up his, well, Air Jordans, and the average NBA player salary is now well over $8 million.

The value that Michael Jordan brought not only to basketball but also to the athletic apparel industry—in particular, Nike's sneaker lineup—is also well-documented. The celebrity sneaker as we know it today is a result of Air Jordans. Jordan's original Nike deal, which he signed in 1984, was for $2.5 million over five years—the most lucrative endorsement deal in all of American sports at the time. As of 2020, Jordan has reportedly earned $1.3 billion from his sneaker endorsements; his 2022 sneaker deal brought him $256 million in one year alone, which is more than double his entire NBA career salary earnings, not to mention it cemented Nike as the undisputed leader in a crowded footwear market.

Although Jordan played a zero-sum game for a living—by their nature, any sports match is zero-sum—his play and notoriety extended well beyond the NBA and permanently broke down barriers for all NBA players to come, allowing them to generate unprecedented wealth. From a broader perspective, off the court Jordan in essence played a non-zero-sum game. We might call such an impact on the market the "Jordan variable," where one person offers so much value that every other player within that market only grows richer. Indeed, during the 1990s, annual growth of the average NBA salary never dropped below 10 percent; it peaked at 21 percent in 1995–1996.[1]

In other words, in a non-zero-sum game, every "player" can enjoy wealth, abundance, enlightenment, or whatever they're playing for, without encroaching on another's success. This is the world we're all playing in.

And not only did the value of Jordan, his NBA peers, NBA franchises, and Nike grow, but also the city of Chicago experienced a boom in tourism and merchandise sales. The Jordan variable boosted the sales of local merchants and the city's tax revenue, sponsorships, and advertising and caused a rising tide in the vicinity of the United Center, where the NBA played, that resulted in greater profits for surrounding restaurants and bars and the creation of new jobs.

Although it's impossible to quantify Michael Jordan's economic impact on Chicago's gross domestic product (GDP) during his reign with the Bulls, it's noteworthy that from 1985, Jordan's rookie year, through 1998, when he retired to try his hand at professional baseball, the Chicago economy boomed year after year. And by the close of the twentieth century, service jobs—the marketing of a service to consumers, such as waiting tables—were permanently driving Chicago's once manufacturing-based economy.[2]

ZERO-SUM

Basketball aside, a *zero-sum game* is any game in which the total gains and losses of all participants balance out to zero. In other words, the sum of one player's gains is equal to the sum of another player's losses. It's both the essence of mergers and acquisitions and the foundation on which the Wall Street financial industry is built. From another perspective, think of zero-sum like poker chips moving around a table. Any benefit obtained by one player is at the direct expense of the other player or players involved, and the total amount of resources or value within the system remains constant. Where do these games play out? Let's move beyond Wall Street for the moment.

In ancient tribal cultures, certain limited resources, such as shelter in a preferred location (perhaps a cave) or rainwater collected for drinking during the dry season, would be considered zero-sum. There is a finite amount of the resource, only so much to go around. In fact, we encounter so many zero-sum games in the media— professional sports, war, financial markets, deluded interpretations of how business is supposed to work—that we've come to believe that's the only game in town. Likely, we evolved as humans with zero-sum games in mind. And it's not really our fault to think this way: our brains operate on ancient circuitries.

Throughout most of human history, people have competed for limited resources. Indeed, most wars historically were fought over resources, whether water, food, timber, oil, minerals, or other essential commodities. One side won, and the other side lost— the conquered most often were liquidated or subsumed under the culture wielding power. Although modern warfare almost always spurs military innovations that often make their way to consumer applications, war on its face, with its target of death, is a zero-sum game (at least as far as the name on the map afterward is concerned).

With the exception of sports matches, war may be the last refuge of the zero-sum Neanderthal.

NON-ZERO-SUM

In contrast, a non-zero-sum game is one in which the total gains and losses of all players involved are not equal to zero. In other words, it's a situation where the outcome is not purely competitive or purely cooperative, but rather creative. In a non-zero-sum game, it's possible for all players to benefit, some to benefit while others lose, or all players to lose, depending on the strategies chosen.

Non-zero-sum games, as we will see, allow for the possibility of collective gains or losses. Cooperation and coordination of players can lead to outcomes where all participants benefit, even if their respective gains may differ. Non-zero-sum games often involve scenarios where players can make agreements, negotiate, or find mutually beneficial solutions. The contemporary, interconnected economy—one now grounded in internet and artificial intelligence—is on its face a non-zero-sum game because the resources offered, such as marketing, sales, and distribution, or the pace of innovation, are boundless, limited only by one's imagination. As Jordan did for sports, every "player" in the modern economy makes the game easier for other players over time.

One obvious example of a non-zero-sum corporate transaction is the partnership between Apple Inc. and Intel Corporation in the early 2000s. At the time, Apple was transitioning its Macintosh computers from PowerPC processors to Intel processors. Apple's decision to switch its hardware architecture naturally presented an opportunity for Intel, the leading semiconductor company of that era.

The benefits of this negotiation for Apple included improvement in performance, which allowed the company to offer consumers faster and more powerful computers. Moreover, Intel processors were widely used in the PC industry, which made it easier for software developers to create applications compatible with both Mac and Windows platforms.

The benefits for Intel were similarly apparent: Apple's decision to switch to Intel not only caused Intel's sales to rocket but also provided Intel with a high-profile endorsement of its technology.

In this collaboration, both Apple and Intel gained advantages without one party's gain being offset by the other's loss. Notably, the success of one company did not come at the direct expense of the other; instead, both parties benefited from the collaboration in terms of technological advancements and market positioning. Value was generated from and received by both sides.

Most importantly, the consumer gained faster personal computer technology and ease of use between Apple and PC products, which in turn advanced productivity in every economic sector.

Non-zero-sum environments are often teeming with creativity. Think of the Italian Renaissance. Certainly, some painters clamored for top-dog status in a narrow field, but the prevalence of and demand for art and culture ran hot enough to enrich more artists, of any level, than ever before.

EVERYONE WINS

We still hear such tired aphorisms as "you eat what you kill" or "there's always a winner and a loser," but these are archaic concepts with roots in a zero-sum mentality. Today, it's a sign of foolishness to believe this still plays out. In truth, all this began to transform with the onset of the Industrial Revolution, which globalized and vastly expanded what previously were, at best, loose networks of local markets. Spanning from the late eighteenth to the mid-nineteenth century, the Industrial Revolution brought about significant changes from predominantly agrarian and hand-made production to mechanized and mass production. Its benefits included the following:

- *Increased productivity:* The introduction of new machinery, such as the steam engine and power loom, and mechanized manufacturing processes led to higher output of goods and a more efficient use of resources.
- *Economic growth:* Industries expanded and created job opportunities in factories, mines, and transportation that attracted people from rural areas to urban centers. The growth of industries also stimulated trade and boosted overall economic activity.
- *Technological advancements:* In addition to steam engines, innovations in iron and steel production, textile machinery, transportation (such as railways and steamships), and communication (such as the telegraph) laid the foundation for future developments and set the stage for subsequent waves of industrialization.
- *Urbanization and improved living standards:* People migrated from rural areas to cities in search of employment. Although urbanization initially led to challenging living conditions, such as overcrowding and poor sanitation, it eventually paved the way for improved living standards. Access to new job opportunities, public services, education, and cultural amenities increased.
- *Expansion of global trade:* The Industrial Revolution sparked a surge in international trade. New technologies

and transportation systems made it easier to transport goods over long distances, facilitating global trade networks.

- *Advances in agriculture:* Innovations in agriculture improved farming techniques and introduced new machinery. Agricultural productivity increased, allowing for higher crop yields and better food production.
- *Social and cultural changes:* This era brought about the rise of labor movements and the push for workers' rights. It also influenced the development of new political, social, and economic ideologies, such as socialism and capitalism, as well as dazzling forms of literature, art, and entertainment.

The modern city was established to provide easy access to human capital, which, because less labor was required, led to more rapid idea sharing and "idea capital." *Idea capital* refers to the intellectual or creative resources, knowledge, and ideas that can be harnessed and leveraged to drive innovation, development, and economic success. It stands for the value and potential of ideas to generate economic or social benefits. Whereas the modern city may have been designed to keep factory workers close at hand, it also produced, among other creative innovations, jazz and pop art—the stuff of cool dorm room posters.

Idea capital may also refer to the investment of resources, such as time, effort, and expertise, into the exploration, refinement, and execution of ideas, with the goal of realizing their full potential. If anything, the market driven by technological innovation today is driven by ideas: *your ideas*, when properly nurtured, supported, and put into motion, are themselves the powerful drivers of progress, growth, and success. And your entry into this infinite market has never been easier, thanks to technology.

In 1820, the average American grew or raised their own food, worked by candlelight, made their own furniture, traveled relatively short distances by horse, and, at best, had a Bible—if they even knew how to read. This was a world where your seven o'clock reservation in the Meatpacking District on Friday night was not the biggest challenge to solve.

Their estimated average household income was in the range of $500 (approximately $13,000 today), an estimate that is probably high because, regrettably, a reported 32 percent of American households in this era also generated income through the efforts of enslaved people. By 1920, some Americans had telephones, some had electricity, and some were starting to travel by gas-powered cars. But income hadn't improved very much: the average US household at the time brought in a little over $1,500 (approximately $23,000 today). Commuter air travel was brand-new and risky, but the early versions of some amenities we have today—radio, film, and consumer electricity—were starting to emerge.

Compare the past two hundred years to our world today: we communicate instantly, in high definition, across thousands of miles with anyone who has a phone or internet connection. We can jet to every corner of the earth. The average annual real household income for Americans is more than $70,000. Most importantly for our interests, we can open a business and reach a boundless, global market with no middlemen, no brick-and-mortar shop, and very little in the way of start-up costs. Technology has demolished all of these previously formidable barriers to entrepreneurship. This doesn't suck—in fact, it's a measure of our growing personal freedom.

THE ECONOMY IS CREATIVE AND EXPANDING

We live in a world that has rapidly accelerated, and the value offered in our free markets is exploding. Thanks to technology, there's a constant expansion of possibility. Even when businesses think they're directly competing against others, they're not. For example, a Pepsi vending machine standing next to a Coca-Cola machine sells more soda than one in isolation because it urges the customer to think, "Do I want a Pepsi or a Coke?" rather than, "Do I want a soda?"

There are very few areas of modern society where the winner takes all—even with existing economic disparity. And so, when it comes to innovation and wealth, we're not playing a zero-sum game anymore. That's because a technological society has very few constraints—there's almost nothing we can't innovate around. If I invent a more efficient microchip and get rich, I didn't take that money from your pocket. In fact, I've *added* money to your pocket by making life more efficient for you in the form of faster computing. Now, your very own digital business is cheaper to launch and scale.

Zero-sum is the world of competition. Non-zero-sum is the world of value and creativity. Competition keeps us right where we were, whereas creativity advances humanity. Competition boils down to rivalry and comparison with individuals or groups in pursuit of a common goal—the emphasis is on outperforming others, gaining an advantage, and ultimately achieving superiority over others. Creativity, on the other hand, is about generating original ideas, concepts, or solutions that are novel, unique, and often divergent from existing norms or conventions. Our modern, technological markets value creativity.

The Really Rich individuals, as I refer to those who understand these mechanics, are aware of this at a deep level because their businesses focus on self-expression, exploration, and innovation. The recent sale of your company for millions, for example, doesn't make anyone green with envy. Your new sports car doesn't inspire a feeling of hatred in others. Why would it? Your business, and even the sale of your business, just made the world richer—either by adding value or by diffusing your resources.

Let's say you record a song, and it becomes a smash hit (certainly something I've attempted and failed at before). Your music entertains and inspires millions, stimulating their respective creative spirits and maybe even offering them hope in dealing with their challenges. The money earned from the song's release keeps the staff at the record company employed, fed, and happy, and the royalties and admiration you earn are your reward for adding value to society.

Or yet another example, this time in business: the sale of your company is the realization of the stored value or processes that you developed. It's not a lotto ticket. You earned it, and society is better for having you build something of staggering value. After your initial public offering (IPO), perhaps even an average person can buy stock in the public company and own a piece of your innovation. Should you really feel guilty about all that?

Maybe you did buy a fancy sports car. Your Italian automobile is fun to drive, and it keeps a storied car manufacturer alive and innovating. The engineers and designers are compensated for their hard work and share in the revenue growth that you've added by purchasing it. A small town in Italy revolves around the sale of more and more of these niche vehicles. Less people go hungry. And around and around we go.

INTERCONNECTEDNESS STIMULATES A NON-ZERO-SUM ECONOMY

From a global perspective, our economy is characterized by interconnectedness and interdependence among nations as well, through trade, investment, and financial flows. Everyone is working together. Economic transactions and interactions generate wealth and value for multiple parties simultaneously. Just as individuals do, when countries engage in international trade, both exporting and importing nations can benefit by specializing in the production of goods or services in which they have a competitive advantage.

More than anything, the gathering AI boom will demonstrate the true extent of a non-zero-sum economic environment. AI technology will automate repetitive tasks, streamline processes, and increase efficiency in various industries. By leveraging AI algorithms and machine learning, businesses and service providers—law firms, for example—will automate mundane and time-consuming activities, which leads to cost savings and increased productivity. Are we really paying lawyers to review boxes of mostly irrelevant documents or instead to think creatively to save your ass in court? This improved efficiency can drive economic growth by encouraging companies to focus on higher-value tasks and innovation, which, again, leads to new opportunities, improved marketing, and new revenue streams.

Those who've amassed wealth and feel a sense of guilt, or those afraid of doing so in the first place, will find solace in a system where what's theirs isn't being pried from the hands of another. And the abundance from the biggest winners in society benefit all in the overall innovation and improvement of quality of life. We all should be thanking them, not pelting them with rotten fruit at press conferences.

The key question—and the first Really Rich behavior—is about creating value. What is valuable in the market, and how does one create such value? *Value*, of course, refers to the worth of usefulness that a good, service, or asset holds for another individual or for society—it's the perceived benefit or satisfaction derived from consuming or owning something. Value runs deeper than blinking computer screens and gobs of hair gel.

The perception of value is naturally subjective and varies from person to person on the basis of their preferences, needs, and circumstances—your brilliant idea today, for example, may not catch on till tomorrow. In the context of a market, value is typically determined through the interactions of supply and demand, meaning the price of a product or service can be influenced by its scarcity, utility, quality, and desirability—you don't have control of every one of these elements. In addition, value isn't fixed or absolute. It changes over time based on consumer preferences, technological improvements, changes in supply and demand, and other factors. Here's a short list of once popular but now devalued products:

- Typewriters
- VHS tapes
- Fax machines
- Floppy disks
- Film cameras
- Pay phones
- Dial-up modems

At one time, someone made a killing on each of these products, as well as on the markets associated with each of these innovations (e.g., Blockbuster). In other words, value is very much a function of time. And the most valuable of ideas always spring from your own creative spirit.

Now that you've gotten a crash course on how the market actually works, let's dive into the first of our ten behaviors for becoming Really Rich.

CHAPTER 2

Create Value

GROW RICH BY MAKING SOMEONE ELSE'S LIFE EASIER

A LL FINANCIAL REWARDS STEM FROM THE SAME ROOT: VALUE. Moreover, the creation of value, which the Really Rich mindset defines simply as *anything that people recognize makes life easier for them*, is the core purpose of a human being. Here is another way of looking at this: the market, or at least your segment of the market, measures how valuable your idea, service, or good is by its response. If no one thinks what you're offering is all that great—meaning, they're not buying it—then your idea holds no intrinsic value.

It's useful to note that *value* in the market isn't a value *judgment*. Creating value isn't necessarily a measure of how many good works you *think* you put out into the world—although, it certainly could be. Rather, if you have a cluster bomb factory and you're in the business of building vicious weapons that kill insurgents, you're creating value in the market to the extent that militaries want to buy what you're offering, no matter how deplorable someone else may think this product is. The only gauge of value in this context is whether people want what you're offering and are willing to pay you for it.

Or maybe you're a dominatrix whipping investment bankers on the Upper West Side of New York, and you're good at it, and certain clients pay big bucks for your services—you're creating value in the market. Not that I've ever enlisted such services, or even recommend it, but who am I to judge? You do you.

Patent leather aside, all commercial transactions, whatever their natures, are deeply embedded in the human experience, and anthropology is replete with evidence of value exchanges.

Tally sticks, for example, are one of the earliest known forms of recordkeeping and were used as a primitive form of currency and accounting in various cultures. Dating back to ancient civilizations in Egypt, China, and Babylon, these were typically made from wooden sticks or bones, with notches or markings carved into them to represent numbers or values. Each stick was split lengthwise, and one part (the stock) was kept by the creditor, while the other part (the foil) was given to the debtor. This ensured a secure record of transactions pertaining to taxes, debts, and other trade—including the earliest forms of credit. Sounds convenient, huh?

From such records, we might observe that exchanges of value were considered to be early evolutionary survival tactics: there's a stored memory of good deeds, and it may be that the social contract is itself founded upon this economic concept of value. When I remember that you helped me yesterday, I'm inclined to help you today. Conversely, if you've helped me but I don't help you when you need me tomorrow, you remove me from the equation. What do you say? "I can't trust him. He doesn't have my back."

If society doesn't pay us back for the value we create, we wouldn't be incentivized to do good, look out for each other, and contribute to the survival of our communities. The very reason we're sitting in apartment buildings and in technological societies is because of the group memory of the good things that a few people have done. And the memory is deep and nearly permanent, whether we had money or not.

Of course, there have always been those who insist that their idea, service, or good is the best, despite the fact that the market—sometimes for decades—disagrees. It's not a crime to have a bad idea. But it is tragic if you fail to iterate your idea, to constantly adjust your offering and your approach, until the market ultimately does respond. There's no glory in toiling over work nobody appreciates. It's also an egotistical endeavor—you're not giving back to the human race. Indeed, devoting your life to something that others find useless is itself a source of pain and confusion in society.

> **Rich:** That's my art! How dare you disrespect it!
>
> **Really Rich:** I'll keep trying new things until someone likes it enough to pay me for it.

Society has always taken this value dynamic very seriously. In medieval Germany, for example, towns developed a certain contraption called an Iron Flute, or a Shame Flute, to humiliate public performers that no one enjoyed. So, if you were considered to be a hack street musician, the town would fit an iron collar around your neck and bind your hands to a flute that would extend down your torso. You couldn't eat, and you had to walk around like that until the village elders figured you'd had enough. It was, literally, sheer torture. It didn't matter how much you liked music or thought you were the next standout flutist—everyone else disagreed. "So, you think you're adding value with these awful songs you're playing? Well, we all disagree and have already tapped the blacksmith on the shoulder about you."

I'm not endorsing corporal punishment, obviously, but I'm making a salient point: the filmmaker who made *what he thinks* is an award-winning movie that no one cares to see, the tech bro who pushed a product to death that no one wants, and the baker who ends up enjoying his own leftover, crappy bread have not created value, despite their lofty ambitions and regard for their own creations. We're not going to fit a steel collar around your neck today, but we are—as a market—going to ignore you. Without a market response, your great idea is no more than a hobby. And, of course, you'll get poorer and poorer over time without changing your approach.

Then again, would a steel collar save you time and nudge you in another direction sooner? It would be a sheer blessing for many.

Perhaps medieval villagers weren't as dumb as we think.

SPECIFIC VALUE

Now, that baker who can't sell his bread may actually be good at baking—perhaps he had a problem with marketing, or maybe where he's from people prefer football-shaped loaves to round rolls. If baking is his thing, and if he's had a vision he can't shake to make this his profession, then he needs to consider what he's currently offering, change something about the recipe, or adjust something about how it's being sold, and try again—in other words, he has to iterate.

People want to own their businesses. In fact, virtually every successful businessperson I've met or interviewed considers their creation to be an amazing feat, one that's appreciated by those who need what they produce. As a result, they're showered both with revenue and status—the only two dynamics with which a market tells an entrepreneur that what they're offering is valued.

When you own your own business, you're at the tip of the spear—a hundred percent of the value you're creating is yours. Of course, you don't pull back 100 percent of your earnings for yourself—you share revenue with everyone in your organization; maybe you pull back 5 percent. But whatever it is, you start with an area of interest to you, you operate within that area of interest, and you keep moving pieces around that board, trying different things until you see something that sticks. Something that lands with the market. This is the practice of iteration, which gives rise to *specific value*.

You can create value in innumerable ways. You can shovel snow, you can move boxes around for people—all that's creating value, and you'll be paid for it. But when you strike a market chord with specific value—something that only you can provide—your profits will multiply exponentially. This is when you get paid the big bucks, when you can leave your car in the middle of the road with the blinkers on and no one screws with you.

Specific value can be sophisticated, or it can be simple—the point is whether a market responds. PayPal was a very sophisticated tech solution that (eventually, certainly not in the first iteration) resonated with the market and sent Elon Musk into a bazillionaire orbit. But you might be an artist who draws authentic, gorgeous chalk figures on playground asphalt and finds thousands, if not millions, of fans online who look for your creations every day. Both products potentially "make life easier" for people, one by letting people sell stuff easily on eBay, and one by filling people with joy. And if they do, both will be rewarded by the market.

Specific value can also be seen as a "market of one." In the past, daunting obstacles stood in your way of developing a market of one. You needed a TV show or an agent, and you probably needed to raise millions of dollars. Now all you need is a few free, discovery-based social media accounts.

The truth is, it's impossible to know how a market will measure your idea and whether what you're offering actually will create value. You can control your creation, but the variable is whether the market will respond. You can't force the market to want you, at least not in a free society. Rather, the market has to voluntarily engage with your idea, and it will if the idea is something people recognize they want.

WORKING FOR A LARGE CORPORATION
DOES NOT PROMISE SAFETY

In America, we're told from birth that we should think for ourselves, that every child has the potential to someday become president of the United States. This is America's greatness: our laws and our culture generally support this mentality of unlimited potential. But do our institutions and systems actually show us how to do this? Or do our schools, instead, train us to be corporate cogs, to function with a herd mentality, to end up working for very large corporations into which we pour far more value than we receive? We're more likely to learn how to be a regional manager than a founder.

Yes, America is most certainly the land of the free and the home of opportunity—as long as you think out of the box and put blinders on to block everything that's being hammered into you. You can grab the fullness of the American Dream; you just have to reject the accepted wisdom and disbelieve the foundations of what you've been told since you were a kid. Is working for a giant tech company or an aerospace behemoth like Lockheed and living behind a white picket fence your American Dream? If it is, knock yourself out. But also consider whether you're being honest with yourself. Certainly, I wasn't when I began my career on Wall Street. It didn't feel quite right from day one.

My dream resembled the arc of futures trader Paul Tudor Jones, who operated out of a four-person office in Connecticut, made millions of dollars, drove around in a stretch limo in a tuxedo, and lived life on his own terms. Obviously, it didn't play out like that when I was trading.

To reach this sort of entrepreneurial American Dream, the Really Rich dream, you have to do everything that you never learned in school. Paul Tudor Jones had no paradigm for his success. His specific-value model didn't even exist yet. He knew he loved trading, and he had a strong hunch he'd be good at it, but everything he initially learned came from the best traders in the cotton trading pits. He went bankrupt multiple times. He then created out of whole cloth the idea of a hedge fund, found investors, took a small percentage of all the fund trades, and made a fortune.

The real American Dream is for the innovators.

The other American Dream is about baseline success: here's your BA or MBA, here's your corporate job—you're not going to be poor, and you'll live in a perfectly nice neighborhood. America will give you a middle-class life on a silver platter. And, of course, if you want to stop there, then stop there. But then again, why did you pick up this book?

We are taught to strive for the middle, in part, by our earliest public schooling—institutions, by the way, that were originally modeled after nineteenth-century Prussian schools designed to raise obedient soldiers for the Prussian army.[1]

But it's the cowboy, the innovator, the iterator who gets the big rewards. Who, when they're young, dreams about the baseline? You're allowed to think big; you're allowed to do crazy stuff that people will insist won't work! You're permitted to make your own rules (just keep 'em legal, kids). In America, you're allowed to behave this way. In America, you can create a product that doesn't exist and then build it and sell it. And, yes, grow very rich, very fast, for your efforts.

The incumbent monolithic American corporations would like nothing more than for you to come work for them rather than you developing a crazy little idea at Stanford and creating a billion-dollar company that competes with them. In America, the monolithic corporation can't kill you, of course, but it can try to buy you for a handsome multiple of your earnings. This should further incentivize all entrepreneurs to hit something out of the park on their own.

You can do just about anything you want. The "boundaries" and the "rules" you're warned about are invisible. Why hasn't anyone told us this?

No one is reaching the American Dream anymore from within the confines of blue-chip corporations, not in situations where you'll toil for forty years and retire and get the million-dollar pension payout and the gold watch. This no longer exists. Moreover, either those blue chips are going to lay you off or you'll quit in two or three years. In today's world, you don't want to stay there, and they don't want you to stay more than a few years anyway: the downsizing is so rapid and mercurial. Why would you play that game when you could play another?

People have a natural desire to create and to own their creations. One of the first things a baby learns to say whether pointing at a stack of toy blocks, a stuffed rabbit, or a human being—every baby—is "Mine!"

LEAD A LIFE OF VALUE AND GET RICH

How do you get your piece of the American Dream—the fancy steak knives with the little bee on them, a garage full of race cars, vacations in tiny Italian coastal villages, or whatever you're seeing in your mind's eye? The answer seems obvious, but few internalize the vision. Almost everyone gets this part backward and asks themselves "How do I make money?" instead of "How can I provide more value?" If you keep asking how to generate the side effect of providing value (money), you're never going to hit on a big idea. You'll simply take advantage of short-lived trends, vulnerable legislation, or mispricing. In other words, you probably will never get Really Rich.

This is why most "get rich quick" books are a waste of time and paper. If you're reading the specifics about how to build a widget with the highest margin, you've already missed it. It's too late. Also, without understanding whether the widget you're concocting offers any form of value to humankind whatsoever, you've lost the battle before you've begun. You'll need to buy the revised edition of that get-rich-quick manual for your next shot on goal.

And another "financial guru" will be happy to charge you for the privilege.

We know that we'll enjoy rewards in proportion to the amount of value we've handed over to society. Solve big problems, receive big awards. Make more lives easier, generate more money. Moreover, you can enjoy these rewards guilt-free because you earned them. There's no need to cower in shame at your good fortune or fill the coffers of the nearest place of worship with gold coins to increase your chances of entering the heavens. You moved the world forward and that's a very good thing. And most of the time, thanks to technology, you'll enjoy the rewards within your lifetime.

PROVIDING VALUE ISN'T EASY

You knew there'd be a catch. So here it is: it won't be easy. You'll need to put in effort—muscle or mental. But, trust me, that's the whole point.

Effort + Receiving Positive Feedback from Something You Care About
= Satisfaction

There's nothing rewarding about inheriting money, becoming famous against your will only to come into large sums of money, or winning the lottery. Some have jokingly referred to hitting the lotto jackpot as a "curse," but, crazy as it sounds, there's something to this notion. You're freeloading on someone else's achievements or you're spending other people's money. Or you just found dumb luck. You didn't learn anything. You didn't break a sweat. You didn't get any closer to understanding reality by revealing a hidden truth. That's why these scenarios often end in tears: bankruptcy, drug abuse, family discord, or even untimely death.

In fact, you don't actually want to get rich quickly.

You *actually do* want to get rich by providing value to other people. And by helping other people, you'll be happier. That takes effort. Money is occasionally dispensed at random, sure, but in the long run it goes to the people providing the most value. There's a reason that Steve Jobs became incredibly wealthy before his death: despite a turbulent career, he made powerful computing smaller and more friendly for everyone to build with and enjoy.

Do you worry about inheritance? Even wealthy families, when their wealth is handed over to their heirs *directly* (instead of being put in a trust, which is managed like a business), end up going broke over time and consume more than they build. The families who stay wealthy have "family offices" or privately owned investment companies that manage only their family's pool of capital. They wisely invest capital that continues to further innovate for society and receive returns on their investments. The snot-nosed son of some industrial titan may be getting a monthly allowance that trumps your yearly salary, but his family's investment capital is creating wealth, even as he wastes a princely sum at the nightclubs in $900 designer sneakers.

On a biological level, the whole "pleasure is in the struggle" dynamic is programmed into our nervous system. That feeling of drive, in the form of dopamine, comes from the struggle and dips at the moment of achievement. There are dozens of studies on this topic for the scientifically minded to pursue.

For example, Dr. Andrew Huberman, a Stanford neuroscientist, uses a football analogy to explain that it's better to skip the touchdown dance and get on to the next play. He argues that if you were to "over-celebrate," you'd feel a drop in dopamine and the victory would strike you as oddly disappointing. An Oxford professor, Mark Walton, is also engaged in fascinating research exploring the biological interactions of dopamine and the human brain to reward effort.[2]

Simply getting handed *anything* without a little struggle is a pretty lackluster experience: *anything* loses its value in the handover.

YOU GET TO DECIDE HOW YOU WANT TO ADD VALUE

Gino, the guy who owns the Italian restaurant on my block, keeps tabs on all his regulars. Without fail, he has a handwritten note on my table upon arrival—"Happy birthday, Nick!" or "Welcome home, Nick!" I enjoy this almost as much as the meatballs—it's monumentally valuable to his customers and keeps them coming back. Want to post funny videos online and build a fan base? Great. Prefer working in a biochemistry lab? All the power to you! Sure, your mom can drive you nuts at Thanksgiving begging you to be a doctor or a lawyer, but if your true passion is making art out of bicycle parts, who cares what Mom says? You're the one who has to do the work.

This is exciting because the world becomes your oyster: try your hand at multiple things to see what sticks best. If you make a mistake and choose a path you think will be exciting just to find it filled with rocks and thorns, you can change course. This applies whether you're fifteen or fifty-five years old.

You're in the driver's seat of how you will provide value. But remember, you must provide value. Sooner or later, you'll have to decide how to do so.

CONFUSED? LOOK TO CHILDHOOD FOR CLUES

Many get stuck at "What should I do?" mostly because they've let so much noise, outside influence, and familial pressure get in the way of their decision-making process. One of the simplest ways to begin refining an area of interest is to identify what came naturally to you as a child before parents, society, media, and big marketing agendas began pushing you around and clobbering you with their ideas.

It's no surprise that entertainers were, as children, the life of family gatherings. Future artists likely have drawers full of elementary school paintings. Scientists probably melted the wallpaper off of their childhood bedrooms once or twice while botching an experiment.

Generally, you can get in the ballpark of what you may be passionate about simply by tracing your passions' roots back to childhood play. I could stay in my room all day and night learning new guitar riffs or writing short stories. Should I be surprised that I bailed on Wall Street only to pursue more creative endeavors? You can only live in denial of your true passions for so long. Otherwise, you risk becoming bitter as you age.

> **Rich:** What did my parents do?
>
> **Really Rich:** What can I uniquely offer?

ONLY THE MARKET DECIDES WHAT'S VALUABLE

Here's where it gets tricky. As we've seen, the market determines what's valuable—not you. Just because you spent your life designing the perfect solar-powered can opener that nobody wants to buy doesn't mean you're due a reward for your efforts. Thinking you deserve a reward without providing value is called entitlement. It's incredibly arrogant to think that *you*, not all of society, know best when it comes to your achievements. If one thing doesn't work out after a while, then pivot and try something new. End of story.

Thousands of start-ups capitalized every year have no market for their products. They're entirely speculative, established on the delusions of the founder and sometimes investors. Some call this an "echo chamber." Cheaply testing the need for your product—with surveys, landing pages, and digital ads—is a way to sidestep the sorrow of spending years of your life on something no one wants. It's critical to get comfortable with accepting the reality of what society demands.

This concept—*iteration*—becomes one of the best ways to approximate what's valuable: you can be "close," and it still appears as though you're failing. Many tech companies started out developing a completely different product than the one they're currently selling, including Slack, PayPal, and Instagram. A heightened sense of awareness can guide you to the winning product as users, founders, and employees gravitate toward one product feature—or complain about another.

WAIT, WHAT'S VALUE AGAIN?

As discussed earlier, value is anything that makes someone else's day better or easier. Of course, I use "someone" loosely—this may be a human, a company, or AI.

What's so exciting about value is that it keeps evolving and the possibilities multiply. You have more opportunities to provide value today (on an enormous scale) than ever before. Especially in entertainment. This is a very good thing.

Take laughter. It's valuable to people and costs nothing but sweat to produce. Historically, if you could make someone laugh, you were well regarded in your community. You were compensated in some small way, whether by being given the privilege of leading gatherings or providing entertainment. Now, with technology, if you can make someone laugh, you can make millions of people laugh, and you have the potential to become a global sensation overnight. Whereas it was impossible to make more than a few thousand people laugh in the 1800s, let alone millions, today your talents coupled with technology equal a bountiful future.

Before the advent of the internet, even professions as low-tech as comedians had far fewer opportunities. Imagine pulling up to a club in New York City in 1985 as a new comedian; your audience might be twenty people max, most of whom don't want to see your show in the first place. Many simply want to ruin your night. Now there are hundreds, if not thousands, of well-paid comedians operating solely online, on podcasts, in merch sites, on private channel memberships, who only occasionally crop up on mainstream television specials and live stages. Even if a tiny slice of the entire world thinks you're funny, you're good to go.

And we keep inventing new things to be good at. Consider blockchain, virtual reality, and scientific and engineering breakthroughs. If you're great at something, you may be world-renowned at that thing in the future. If you're a therapist sitting in your office, imagine extending your practice to anyone around the world with virtual or augmented reality, where both patient and therapist feel as if they're in the same room. If you're not excited yet, reread this passage. The future is a place of expanded opportunities to provide value. Your life can get far, far better no matter where you currently stand.

Rich:	*That's* your job?
Really Rich:	Why not?

WHAT'S VALUABLE DOESN'T
STAY STATIC OVER TIME

Of course, some value opportunities degrade and can later disappear altogether. Driving a bus, for instance, is a valuable job today (getting people safely to and fro), and your municipality is happy to provide you with a salary and benefits. But in the not-too-distant future, a robot will be taking the wheel. That's not a net good initially for bus drivers (the part), but it's a net good for humanity (the whole)—travel will become safer and cheaper and will operate around the clock. Robots don't need a coffee break, nap, or health insurance.

As the financial thinker and hedge fund manager Ray Dalio has said, "Nature optimizes for the whole, not for you."

So, moving people safely will always be valuable (at least until teleportation disrupts that market), but the service you provide as a bus driver will likely degrade and disappear. And that's okay.

Eventually, bus drivers will find another way to support the transportation industry (maintaining robots or providing specialized customer service, for instance) or they'll follow a new passion in another industry. I'm sure a handful of bus drivers love driving their bus (many more seem like they don't enjoy it very much), but they'll make themselves useful elsewhere eventually. Rapid change is a constant in modern society.

Embrace it.

> **Rich:** Don't reinvent the wheel.
>
> **Really Rich:** Tomorrow won't look like yesterday.

VALUE IS TIME-DEPENDENT

All this suggests that you can be too early when providing ground-breaking value to society—or you may be too late. Indeed, the value provided may take some time for a population to appreciate and reward, much to your frustration.

"Too late" is perhaps the most obvious. Perfecting the vinyl record player in 2023 may be an innovation that's too late, save for a few indie audiophiles living in Brooklyn. Digital music has long replaced vinyl, with vinyl occupying a tiny fraction of the overall music industry revenues.

In business and tech, many will remember the proliferation of various blockchain technologies that piled on during the crypto boom of 2021–2022. Even though developers improved on the basic idea popularized by Bitcoin, few were able to achieve significant market share, and many, such as Solana (touted to be a superior tech to Ethereum, another blockchain technology), crashed by more than 90 percent. These products missed the chance for mainstream adoption, and it had nothing to do with the quality of the infrastructure. In this case, the first mover retained all of the advantages (and still does at the time of writing).

Similarly, as investors, traders, and teens lost faith in underlying cryptocurrencies, products built on top of the blockchain, such as nonfungible tokens (NFTs), took a more spectacular tumble. In fact, the daily trading value of OpenSea, the largest NFT exchange, hovers around $5 million at the time of writing, down from upward of $500 million. Minting a new NFT collection in 2025 is more likely to yield laughs than windfall profits.

On the other hand, "too early" also applies to the companies that make the first iteration of a game-changing technology. Often the first isn't always the best, such as the MP3 audio player embedded in pretty much anything with storage space these days. Few remember Diamond Multimedia's "Rio" sound player, the world's first portable MP3 player, but the history books won't miss the iPod or iPhone, which perfected this handheld technology for many millions of people within a decade.

A well-known example of poor timing would be the painter Vincent van Gogh, whose immense cultural value was only fully recognized after his death. In life, he was near broke. I would argue that a contemporary van Gogh would be "discovered" within his lifetime and be found living in Soho in fancy digs thanks to social media and rapid information exchange. Unfortunately, and not to minimize van Gogh's probable mental illness, the real van Gogh didn't get to enjoy the fruits of his labor while he was alive, given the communications technology of his day.

> **Rich:** Nobody appreciates me.
>
> **Really Rich:** I must be working on the wrong thing.

ANYTHING THAT MAKES MONEY BUT DOESN'T PROVIDE VALUE IS THEFT

You can make money in a nearly unlimited variety of ways, but not all of them provide value. Some methods take advantage of legal loopholes, political connections, and information asymmetry. This is scamming your way to wealth, and even if it's legal, it's not sustainable.

Let me be clear: anything that produces income for you that doesn't advance society is theft. Even in the gray areas of providing value, such as financial arbitrage, an industry toward which many individuals like to angrily point their fingers, value is provided in closing price gaps or discrepancies in the financial markets. Of course, once the arbitrage squeezes mismatching prices together, there's no more money to be made for anyone in the long run.

However, winning a government contract because you have a politician in your pocket, selling tainted baby formula that you produced on the cheap to undercut the competition, or using high-pressure sales tactics to sell fraudulent securities is a surefire way to pull value out of society.

Those who transact in these corners of society and get away with it find that after the loophole is closed (and it always closes eventually), they're left with very few options to continue earning similar income. At the time of writing, those who profited from building valueless NFT and digital collectible schemes are guilty of this fallacy. They may have made a few million bucks "tricking" an audience into thinking their art was valuable, but they'll never be able to continue the enterprise in the long run. Many end up broke, in jail, or scrambling for the next scam. Why waste your time in the first place?

Unfortunately, these schemes entrap a disproportionate number of young individuals. I certainly didn't have a clear vision of what was providing real value and what was simply ripping people off when I was fresh out of high school—I was too concerned about making money no matter what. The truth is that a long-term mindset only comes with weathering a few "years in the market."

If you return to the core question "What can I do to provide value?" when you're looking to increase your income, you'll virtually sidestep this trap altogether. If you know you can get rich just as easily by helping people, why put any effort into scamming them?

> **Rich:** Anything for a buck.
>
> **Really Rich:** It's an empty trend. I'll look elsewhere.

ANYTHING THAT DOESN'T CONTINUE
TO PROVIDE VALUE WILL DIE

If what you do doesn't provide value or will soon no longer provide value, you can assume your rewards are about to disappear. Legislation is valuable. Lawyers are valuable. However, many aspects of being a lawyer are degrading in value. For example, lawyers who charge high rates for manual document review (almost always performed by junior hires working for a higher-earning senior partner) will be replaced by AI robots programmed with the entire legal canon. Simply, technology will do a better job at document review than a junior hire prone to mistakes and whiskey hangovers. Lawyers should be compensated for their creativity, not for robotic reviews. It's clear that document review, as a profit center for lawyers, will degrade and eventually die.

If you understand and internalize this phenomenon, you can get ahead of the curve.

When I was coming up in my career, the pit traders (people who literally shouted transitions back and forth at each other) on the Chicago Board of Trade fell into two categories: those who lived in utter denial that computerized trading was coming (and eventually found themselves without work) and those who made the change to working in the new computerized trading world. The many left behind were unable to earn a fraction of the income they'd enjoyed as traders. A not-so-funny quip during the computerized transition was that the once gold-Rolex-wearing pit traders were now driving taxis. These guys simply couldn't comprehend that their skills would become obsolete within their lifetimes.

Even as I designed my trading algorithms at large investment banks, I felt that a robot was coming for me soon or, at the very least, a new, user-friendly technology for our clients that would be cheaper than keeping my expensive ass on the payroll. Now, sophisticated algorithmic trading strategies are available to nearly everyone, including small retail investors, via new crypto start-ups and open-source code. Nineteen-year-old kids have the same algorithms on their Mac that took me and a team of developers hundreds of thousands of dollars to build and deploy on my desk on Wall Street. Now you can rent them for twenty dollars a month.

Of course, there's always an exception to the rule. Things become strange when the state gets involved in supporting dying industries. Governments can and do attempt to put no-longer-valuable jobs on life support to please their constituencies, win votes, and further ulterior motives. Such government spending rarely generates long-term returns, is inflationary to local currency, and only bides time before an even worse crash occurs. It's the equivalent of sticking a piece of chewing gum in a crack in the Hoover Dam. It bastardizes the entire free market economy and leads to more tears than letting the thing break in the first place.

Examples of government boondoggles like this abound—look no further, for example, than the American steel industry. Twenty years ago, as more and more steel was produced more cheaply over-seas, the government flooded the steel industry with enormous sub-sidies before Bethlehem and US Steel, among others, sank like the *Titanic*. A more recent failure was Solyndra, a solar energy company that went bankrupt in 2011 despite being stuffed with $500 million in taxpayer funds.

Markets should allocate capital—not bureaucrats, because when they do, zombie businesses roam the earth.

The death of outdated structures makes way for new, more effi-cient, sturdy, and valuable systems. Subsidizing things that should have died years ago limits an entire population from relearning and becoming valuable again and undermines the humanity of those involved by rewarding stagnation rather than creativity.

> **Rich:** It's my job.
> **Really Rich:** Here's what I offer.

HIGHER CREATIVITY, HIGHER VALUE

Quite possibly one of the most valuable things you can do for someone else in the winter is shovel snow off their driveway. It's a straightforward and uncomfortable job. Most able-bodied people with a jacket and gloves can handle the task. You'll be paid for your time and sweat, not for racking your brain.

Well, combining heating coil technology and paving expertise so that the driveway doesn't collect ice and snow in the first place is a big, more creative step. Now you'll be able to supply developers, commercial buildings, and new homeowners with a shovel-free win-ter. You'll service far more homeowners at once. The company that you've built to market and deliver this technology may make you rich.

You'll often see that emerging electric vehicle manufacturers blow past legacy automakers by making their own electronics and devices to elevate the status quo of driving. Of course, they could simply replicate the conventional car dashboard using components that already exist. But what happens is the added creativity boosts the driving experience for new EV drivers, making it seem foolish for them to return to operating a traditional, run-of-the-mill automobile. In this way, EV manufacturers make it even harder for less-innovative incumbents to catch up.

Creativity leads to innovation, which leads to providing more value at scale at a lower and lower price.

> **Rich:** They won't pay a penny more.
>
> **Really Rich:** Overdeliver and they won't even ask for a receipt.

YOU WILL NEED TO BE MORE CREATIVE TO OFFER VALUE IN THE FUTURE

Robots take the crappy jobs first. Redundant factory work is dehumanizing—we're happy to let a bot take over, as much as labor unions will complain in the near term. Then, waste disposal. Then, the really dangerous things, like bomb disposal and even remote military missions. Then, unskilled transportation and logistics. Then, copywriting, summarizing, rote memorization, and error checking.

With technology, one person's creative breakthrough can be coded and replicated infinitely, affording the entire human race its benefit. The inventor is rewarded both directly and indirectly by society's "upgrading." The average person is rewarded indirectly in the form of the efficiencies unlocked with the new technology. Everybody wins when microprocessors get cheaper and faster. However, new ideas must be continually generated for the creator to be rewarded directly.

Communication technology eliminates "bubbles of innovation" and instantly spreads the findings globally. In ancient Japan, entire towns were dedicated to the manufacture of specialty goods, such as swords or pottery. The technical skill was physically condensed into these regions and kept secret from those outside the city walls. Not so today with consumer technology that can be replicated rapidly and cheaply and shipped almost instantaneously around the world.

Nevertheless, although there are already AI "painting" technologies that take several inputs from humans and blend together images found on the internet for something "new," robots still don't make decisions on their own.

Human originality will be the last thing the robots replace. Position yourself accordingly.

WHAT IF I'M NOT A CREATIVE PERSON?

The value I'm exploring, again, isn't market value—the current price at which an asset or service is bought and sold. It's also not limited to brand value or social value. If anything, the value the Really Rich seek to provide is a sort of utility value—the measure of how much satisfaction, ease, or happiness a consumer can gain from your product or service.

Similarly, the creativity I refer to here isn't necessarily that of Renaissance painters or ballet choreographers but that of problem solvers—specifically, problem-solving that doesn't require a wrecking ball or team of experts. A creative solution is always simple, cheap, and effective. Often, it's not the *common* solution, which is why I call it out as creative. It's way simpler and objectively dumber than the common solution. As Nassim Nicholas Taleb, the author and mathematician, has said, "If stupid works, it's no longer stupid."

In every practice, including seemingly cut-and-dried subjects like mathematics, creativity is involved. Many creatures in the animal kingdom display creativity, but none to the extent that humans do. Beyond consciousness, creativity is our superpower, capable of saving us from every impending doom scenario imaginable, from asteroids to famine and fuel shortages. We can come up with creative solutions to escape unscathed and stronger for having solved the problem in the first place. I rest easy knowing that if a comet was hurtling toward Earth, someone would figure out how to knock it off its warpath of death, and I can get back to sipping my coffee.

EXERCISE

List at least three things that come easy to you that others struggle with (e.g., mathematics, a performing art, or, even, listening):

_____

_____

_____

Order these three things by how much you enjoy doing them or
note which of these you're already doing for fun in your free time:

_____

_____

_____

Which of these activities have you observed made someone's life
better, easier, or more entertained (e.g., through compliments,
social media following, local notoriety you've received)? When has
someone thanked you profusely?

_____

_____

_____

CHAPTER 3

Give the Market
What It Wants

YOU DON'T DECIDE WHAT'S VALUABLE

WORKING IN FINANCE DURING THE FINANCIAL CRISIS IN 2008 was for me, shall we say, a rare pleasure. The bank I was working for in 2009 acquired Lehman Brothers from bankruptcy for pennies on the dollar. The shake-up was so extreme in my group that my managing director (my boss) was demoted, and I was transferred to another department.

I had never met the new head honcho before he showed up and unceremoniously cleaned house. Another intern stood in awe of this guy's omnipresence on the desk at all hours, but I was horrified: his day-to-day life was my worst nightmare—up before the crack of dawn just to take a train and "manage" a bench of insanely money-hungry twenty-somethings. Naturally, I verbalized this sentiment to the intern next to me. It went something like this:

> **Me:** Can you believe this clown is stuck here with us at
> this hour?

Him: Watch what you're saying. You'll want to be him one
day. He's an MD!

Me: Be him? I'd rather be anywhere but here. When I'm
his age, I'll be on a beach in the South of France.

Him: Then why are you still here?

I didn't have a good answer.

Having a clear example of what we *don't* want is just as helpful
as knowing what we *do* want. Because who wants to waste their life
and their time with things that don't interest them?

I know it's not easy to walk away from a mid-six-figure job. Still,
when I got out of college, I wasn't doing anything original. I merely
chose the highest-paid option from the cardboard-cutout lives on
offer upon graduation. When I showed up for work every day, it
looked a lot like yesterday.

In Japan, they'd refer to me as a salaryman. In America, a wage
slave. These are dirty words.

Yet I clung to my job title and brand-name clothing like life support. This was the false comfort and security of a high-salary job,
but it was eating away at my soul. Two things became apparent as I
slogged my way through my career as a trader:

1. Technology was going to replace me.
2. I didn't like what I did enough to make it worth any
   amount of money they could have handed me.

By 2016, after I had quit my job, completed my blues-band odys-
sey, and got back on my financial feet selling résumé prep to executives, I had arrived in Miami. There, I saw something completely

new. No one I was associating with had a fancy degree, an MBA, or a cookie-cutter career trajectory. And, miraculously, they had way more money than my friends in New York. They drove better cars. Took better vacations. They treated themselves with more respect, from the way they decorated their homes to how they celebrated each other's accomplishments. It seemed on all counts that they lived fuller lives.

How could this be?

Well, here is where I found the keystone: they had tried lots of different things that they already enjoyed and didn't quit until something worked. And when it worked, they went all in. That's when they won big. Most importantly, they were comfortable with uncertainty.

The corporate model that the New York financial world offered me works for millions of people, and I hold nothing against them. It just didn't work for me.

Ask yourself if where you are now works for you.

THE MARKET IS YOUR GAUGE

You can choose to do whatever you like in life but without the guarantee that you'll be rewarded. That's because society—"the *market*," not *you*—gets to decide what's valuable and what it wants to receive from you.

Society has an enormous, unquenched desire for *value*. Value comes in all shapes and sizes. If an individual can tap directly into a need, accidentally (most likely) or intentionally (unlikely), then he or she will experience great rewards, either monetary profit or admiration—often both. This is the market rewarding them, often without warning.

Now, of course, we each have to try to figure out what our market is before we launch, but more often than not we learn, via broad market feedback, that our first idea wasn't exactly right. And even when we think we know our market, we'll end up collecting a lot more information in real time.

For example, most technology companies started out as something else. Two former employees of Yahoo! created WhatsApp in 2009 as an early iPhone app that would display user status in a phone's Contacts that showed whether a person was at work or on a call. How stimulating. Six months after launch, the app had merely a handful of users, and one of the founders was considering a new job. But later, it morphed into an instant-messaging service— through no intent of its founders—and within another couple months had a quarter million users. Today more than two billion people use the service—now we're talkin'.

Instagram began in 2010 as an app known as Burbn, designed to be a mobile check-in service. Observing, however, that Foursquare had already launched a similar service (whoops!), the founders refocused their app on photo sharing, which had become an unexpectedly popular feature among its users. They renamed it Instagram, and the app, as we know, exploded. Today, it has 1.2 billion users worldwide. And, well, how many of you are still using Foursquare?

PayPal, for its part, launched in 1998 as Confinity, a company envisioned to develop security software for handheld devices. But the market did not respond, and Peter Thiel, along with other cofounders, completely reimagined Confinity—soon to be PayPal—to focus on electronic payments and digital wallet development. Turns out, making it easier to buy stuff on this new thing called the internet was a big deal.

YouTube started—but failed—as an online video dating service. And on it goes.

The point is that the history of each of today's major tech companies proves two truths: (1) almost no one gets it right the first time; and (2) every successful entrepreneur observes and learns from market feedback and retools their focus. Once you enter the market, you start to iterate within your own idea, market philosophy, or service to hone a perfect match, which you couldn't have ever seen without, so to speak, playing in the field. That's because absolutely no one, ever, can be sure how a market will respond. The market will instruct you, and if you listen like a humble student, it will tell you where to go.

> **Rich:** Hear me out! You don't understand!
>
> **Really Rich:** I'll listen first.

THE EXPLOSIVE MARKETPLACE

As a result of technological developments within social media, there's been no better time in history when we could test a product or service in a broad market and gain relatively immediate feedback as now. Within only one generation, we no longer need to depend on middlemen—agents, brokers, inside connections, and the like—to bring our unique offerings to large numbers of consumers. Often, for many goods and services, in fact, we need no more than a social media account. We can directly reach the end user of our product or service from our mom's basement. The technological infrastructure is that damned good.

The agent or broker "gatekeeper" is increasingly irrelevant, because each individual now has an opportunity to directly gauge the intelligence of a mass audience. In the 1980s, for example, two or three people would decide whether your book or record had any value, and if they decided it didn't, then you had precious few options. Famously, the rock band Lynyrd Skynyrd was turned down by numerous record executives; meanwhile, in live performances, audiences were going berserk for their "too long for radio" song "Free Bird." And, of course, even the Beatles were initially turned down by the Decca label. So, who knows best? The "expert" or the market?

Today, many thousands of writers, recording artists, comedians, entrepreneurs, and other service providers from all over the world—whether in entertainment or not—have broken through on social media platforms and quickly ramped up to successful outcomes way beyond what they imagined. In part, this phenomenon encapsulates a very clear dynamic: a broad, accessible market is always a better determinant of value than two or three individual gatekeepers. The more people there are evaluating your product, the more accurate is the representation of value the market perceives you're creating because consumers—not gatekeepers—have their hands on what you're offering, and they're engaged with it.

In this sense, the scale of market testing has exponentially increased. We no longer depend on the subjective biases and tastes of a few people. Accordingly, when hundreds and then thousands of people weigh in, we can clearly see what's working and what isn't. This is a blessing if you're willing to suspend judgment.

The measure of a market's response is also more objective because of the social identity dynamics of a crowd. People in crowds—especially anonymous people in social media crowds—identify with shared causes or affiliations, enhancing group cohesion and motivation. It's this dynamic, together with what's known as a crowd's "emotional contagion," that in part prompts a product or phenomenon to go viral. The good stuff is recognized in an enormous wave that sweeps across a market with more power than anything comparable historically.

Merely one or two generations ago, you might have had to market your product for a year or more, receive (if you were lucky) a few dozen no-thank-yous, and resort to believing in yourself while you sat there and considered what the hell to do next. Product development and promotion took many years.

What we have now, instead, is an environment of rapid feedback, with shorter and shorter loops providing intelligence on what's working and what's not. This condensed timeline means we get a lot more at bats: we have so many more opportunities to iterate throughout the course of our lives as opposed to what we were facing even twenty years ago. You can determine whether your business will survive in an afternoon with a simple landing page and a paid social media ad.

We're no longer constrained by a lack of market-related technology or an archaic mode of transmitting ideas. Back in the day, not only was it costly to get ideas out but it was also slow. You developed a new software? Great, there's this annual symposium of developers held in New York or San Jose in June. Can't get there? It's months away? Too bad; that's the pace of the market. Well, today you can disseminate your idea as soon as tomorrow and virtually for free.

Markets, of course, are fickle and subjective. A silly product known as the Pet Rock (an actual rock packaged as a toy for kids) worked in 1975 and earned a reported $4 million (currently, about $23.5 million) for the advertising executive who created it, but such a product may not catch a market's fancy today. Still, subjectivity is naturally flattened on social media because an idea is presented to many thousands of people—not just buyers at Mattel or Hasbro. And the feedback we get is much more accurate: if it's not working at scale, then it's very likely not going to work.

There is, of course, a certain groupthink mechanism at play on social media networks. People can go wild for your product, or they can slam you—at the extremes, you can produce a cascade of opinion that could either make you or bury you practically before you've even launched. But think of it like this: If there's a cube sitting in the middle of a room and one person eyeing it from their lone perspective, that person might see a corner or a flat side and misjudge the shape of the whole object. After all, a cube looks quite different in two dimensions, depending on where you're standing. But if a hundred people in the room circle around the cube and look, there arises a deep understanding of the contours of the cube—especially when everyone's talking about what they see. Reality is a complex, unpredictable business. The more vantage points we have, the more likely it is to be viewed from an honest, realistic perspective. Truth is the cube. Different perspectives will get you to the truth.

The algorithms of social media promote things that users have determined to be most interesting. The more intriguing your product, the more engagement you'll have; the more engagement you have, the more people you'll reach: this is the bet that social media makes. If a few people are intrigued by something, the engines that drive social media anticipate that others will find it appealing as well. Indeed, this is not only the inherent nature of the social media phenomenon but also a reflection of how markets naturally evolve—it's just that now it's happening at a lightning-fast pace.

> **Rich:** I know what they want.
>
> **Really Rich:** Let's ask our customers first.

IT PROBABLY WON'T WORK AT FIRST

Now, if your idea isn't resonating with your anticipated audience, you can do one of two things: you can wait until the time matures, or you can revise your idea.

Often, it's not so much that your idea isn't a good one—and we will discuss what constitutes a good idea later—but that you're not positioning it right. Perhaps you're misidentifying your market. Perhaps you're not expressing what you have to offer in an entertaining or clear way. There are numerous paths to promote a product or service, and almost always choosing the right one requires experimentation and multiple attempts. I'm sure there are some out there who get it right on the first try, but I don't think I've ever met any of them.

Of course, not everyone is capable of listening to the market. I'm not suggesting you need to be some sort of savant, but laziness might get in the way. Usually, the challenge is a matter of ego. How many authors, songwriters, or filmmakers do you know who remain attached to their so-called big break that for years has not caught fire? If I had continued to grind away in my band in New Orleans, I can all but promise you that you wouldn't be reading this book.

Look, I know it's hard to change what you just built and thought was such a great idea, but everything has to evolve. Even your idea that's good for a while won't be good forever—companies like Apple, for example, continue to innovate. They can either roll out new products or stay satisfied with slower, less efficient iPhone models—which do you think the market prefers? The fact is, Apple isn't foisting better products on the market, but rather the needs and preferences of the market are changing, and that causes Apple to adapt.

Understanding this model provides a sense of security. You know that you're not going to get it right straightaway, that things are going to go wrong, and that your first iteration isn't going to work. People won't want your burger quite the way you think they will; not until you accidentally try shredded cheese when you run out of sliced will people go nuts. But if you're open and honest and accept the market's feedback, you will eventually find your way. The key is to believe that everyone else, meaning the market, knows better than you do.

When you enter the market, ask yourself what you're trying to achieve and whether it's going in the right or wrong direction. Do you want eyeballs on your product? Sales? Demos? Press mentions? In other words, what metric is right for what you're offering? In which area will the market provide its most effective feedback?

The funny thing is that, in the beginning, you may have no idea what your metric is! So play with different metrics. And if you hear nothing but crickets across the board, you absolutely will have to change something.

Some people are terrified by social media because they don't have a bazillion followers yet and wonder how in the world the market will find them. Well, that's a partly valid worry, but again, considering social media algorithms, start slow, get some traction, and if you do, you'll find that the market finds you. About two weeks before I posted my first Rich vs. Really Rich video, I didn't even have a TikTok account; by the end of my first week on TikTok, I had acquired millions of plays, and I was off and running.

The product you're offering is everything. We all know the example of the terrific pizza place that has perpetually dirty tables and the guy behind the counter is a murderous-looking goon, but you're still there lining up out the door and down the block. Why is that? Because the pizza is great—the product is a knockout. Who cares about anything else?

As I've alluded to, the market "votes" in two ways: with money and/or with admiration. As for the latter, impressions might lead to fame, but fame doesn't always result in profits. In fact, in our digital age, fame is cheap and often disconnected from profit. Instead, you have to "turn on" that celebrity into something that people want to buy. What do you do with your notoriety? Sell T-shirts? Offer a course or a coaching program? Market stuffed dumplings? Well, you could have mad fame on social media, but if those dumplings suck, no one is going to buy them.

Receiving market feedback is the most critical element of success. Interestingly, Sam Altman, the founder of OpenAI, defines *burnout* in a novel way—it's not just working really hard too much, he says, but it's working really hard *and getting no positive feedback*. That's what'll kill you. If you're not getting the "applause" from the market—in either sales or admiration—there's no question that something has to change. You'll be glad when you start getting applause elsewhere, trust me.

Rich:	It just has to work out.
Really Rich:	If it doesn't work out soon, I'll make adjustments.

DON'T WORRY ABOUT OPPORTUNITY

Making money is all about spotting opportunities, right? But *opportunity* is a tricky word—it's commonly misunderstood to suggest that it's somewhere "out there" rather than *in here*. Each opportunity is unique, each an opening for your special disposition and experience rather than a hole in the market anyone could fill with a unique product or service. In other words, an opportunity that you cannot address isn't an opportunity to you—it's noise.

Let's think about it like this: If you saw that the LA Lakers were in need of, say, a better point guard, someone who could really facilitate stronger offense for the team and lead them to another championship, does it mean that *you* should step up for the job? Even if you'd like to jump into the role of point guard because you've been shooting free throws in your backyard for years, you wouldn't be able to do it without a lifetime of high-level, competitive basketball experience. Identifying an "opportunity" is useless unless you can specifically fill it. I'm willing to bet that fewer than 1 percent of those reading this book can dunk on an NBA hoop!

Alternatively, perceiving an opportunity that anyone could fill isn't an opportunity at all. This is the comical landscape of social media "business content." That's simply a game of musical chairs. Any scheme or opportunity with no barriers to entry will be immediately filled—this is why selling on Amazon and drop-shipping have plenty of "players," but few make money because they compete directly against each other (their products are identical, made by the same factory in China) and drive profit to zero. The only ones making money are those who teach others about drop-shipping! Social media is filled to the brim with talking heads spouting information about so-called *obvious* money-making opportunities, but these tips are about as useful as telling you to stand in on point guard for the Lakers.

So don't worry about market opportunities. Focus on your unique role in adding value to the world—the qualities or skills that only you can provide. In fact, it would be better had you never heard about the "opportunity" in the first place because it has (1) wasted your time and (2) distracted you from your interests.

> **Rich:**　What's hot?
>
> **Really Rich:**　What do I do best?

UNDERSTAND WHO YOU ARE

You were born with both a unique disposition and a perspective that your life experiences have helped shape. If you were singularly special at birth (which you were), you're even further distinguished by your lived experience. Therefore, right out of the gate, you're valuable. The trick is identifying your unique aspects and applying them to a world that's hungry for solutions.

You can engage the discovery process by asking others how they'd describe you and digging through your past interests and passions (even the ones you've tossed aside). This step is nonnegotiable because it will save you from attempting unfulfilling tasks and endeavors that rob you of precious time.

To find your unique viewpoint, you may

- Revisit your childhood or early teen hobbies
- Ask your closest friends "what you'd be good at"

- Take a personality assessment
- Actively visualize dream or ideal scenarios

I suggest keeping a notebook of your responses to these activities; their clarity will improve over time. Because without knowing who you are and what you want, you will be hard-pressed to find a way forward.

Additionally, you may want to explore the following:

- What combination of traits and interests make you one of a kind (e.g., the lion-taming ballet dancer)?
- In what way are you best able to communicate your ideas (music, visual art, writing, speech, etc.)?
- Who in the real world do you admire and why? List their characteristics.

When you know who you are, you can narrow down the best paths forward with more accuracy. When you don't know who you are, every step is a blind gamble.

BECOMING REALLY RICH IN THE MARKET

I want to be clear: not everyone has to be an entrepreneur to enjoy the lifestyle of the Really Rich. Some who dream of healing others become doctors and may indeed find themselves Really Rich within the bureaucratic, administrative confines of a hospital. Others want nothing more than to be teachers, and they spend their careers feeling Really Rich in large schools or educational districts. Just don't be a teacher if you really want to be a corporate raider and vice versa.

The process of becoming Really Rich, therefore, isn't limited to entrepreneurship, and it certainly isn't limited to what I, or anyone else, think that you should do. It's really your call.

What Really Rich is most about is being true to yourself. If you know, deep down, that you want to be an artist, then fight for that and continue to reinvent that passion. If you're more like me, and you love to build businesses and make money, then do that. On the other hand, if you love the law but deep down believe you don't fit in a corporate law firm on a partner track, find another way to express yourself in the market. Really Rich is the coupling of your unique creative spirit with the realities of the marketplace. The result is personal freedom, and that's what will separate you from the merely rich.

This is not easy to accomplish, but it's a certain road to success. What it takes is iteration—the ability to reinvent yourself and your product, the wisdom to listen to and adapt to the market, and the courage to stay true to your path.

EXERCISE

Review the list of traits and interests you set forth at the end of Chapter 2.

What uncommon combinations of traits make you unique or potentially make you one of a kind (for example, you're a sculpture artist while working as a big-rig truck driver!)?

_____

_____

_____

In which settings have you garnered the most attention up to now (it could be school, work, sports, the gym, a comedy club)?

_____

_____

_____

What have you not tried yet, or where have you not tried it, that may expose new people to your ideas and skills?

_____

_____

_____

Who do you most admire and how are they garnering attention? What new thing would you be willing to try?

_____

_____

_____

CHAPTER 4

Iterate Forever

TINKER AND REINVENT UNTIL SOMEONE STARTS CLAPPING

CONSIDER THE STORY OF HAMDI ULUKAYA, THE FOUNDER OF multibillion-dollar yogurt behemoth Chobani. Ulukaya was a stateless immigrant upon landing in the United States in 1994 as a twenty-one-year-old who could not speak English and did not know a soul in his new country. He had been a student and a young journalist in Turkey but was compelled to leave as a result of his public criticisms of the Turkish government. Well, once in the United States, he couldn't realistically make a living as a journalist in an English-speaking country, so he had little choice but to reflect upon what else he knew how to do. And he had to think fast, because he had no money.

He and his family used to make cheese on a rural farm in Turkey. Figuring he at least knew how to do that, he secured work in cheese factories among his first jobs in America. After some few years passed, he noticed that a failing yogurt factory in upstate New York was offered for sale. If he knew how to produce cheese, how hard would it be to make yogurt instead? He managed to buy that factory, preserved the jobs of the grateful employees, and, through innovative management techniques, ultimately grew his business into the largest Greek yogurt producer in America.

Ulukaya, of course, did not at first set out to be a yogurt mogul, and he had no blueprint for what he was doing—for all he knew, at the time, Greek yogurt in the United States would be a flop. So, he had to test the market, listen to what it said, and iterate his product, his manufacturing costs, and his sales strategies accordingly. Seems pretty simple from this vantage point, doesn't it?

His story suggests that although the market gets to decide what's valuable, it won't rule you out altogether because you—everyone, really—have an unlimited variety of things to offer. Iteration, a cyclic process of making adjustments and improvements based on market feedback and experience, doesn't take intelligence, money, or connections. Rather, it takes only persistence and a little creativity. Even if you're sitting in a high-paid job, you should consider thinking like Ulukaya and from time to time ask yourself, "What can I offer?" You may be surprised by the answers that present themselves.

This is not a new idea, but it's remarkable to me that virtually no university business program drills this into students. Eric Reis's "Lean Startup" methodology, for one, notes that "rapid iteration" encourages entrepreneurs and businesses to build minimal versions of their products, measure the performance, learn from user feedback, and then iterate quickly to improve. Although this wouldn't exclusively lead anyone to becoming Really Rich, it is nevertheless a critical behavior.

Let me dispel a common misconception: iteration is not settling for less or trying a path that's a major bummer to you; it's changing the plan to something different but equally rewarding. Iteration also puts the wielder on the good side of luck. By trying lots of different things, you unlock opportunities for serendipity. Most of medicine's biggest discoveries, from penicillin to blood thinners, were the results of iteration, so much so that the machine learning and AI tech that powers Big Pharma is designed to do just that—iterate—as rapidly as possible.

The process of iteration is a surefire way, over time, to land on something meaningful as well as rewarding that anyone at any stage of life can exploit.

THERE'S ALWAYS A WAY OUT OF HELL

When you're building something new, whether it's art or a business, there's no framework for how to keep it going when it's working or not working, how and when to pivot, and how long to stick around before bailing out. But with each iteration, the market will always respond. When your idea works, you'll know it because you're awarded either profit or attention. And that's the direction you head toward. But if it's not working, the concept of iteration suggests you make a change as opposed to continuing down the same road.

Instead of saying, "Well, I'll just keep at it," or "I'll draw on my sweat and grit and determination to stay here in this painful place," you have to adjust. You won't do it exactly the way you first conceived of it; as a matter of fact, by the time the market showers you with applause, you might not even have the same idea or product that originally inspired you. And that's okay!

Iteration is the sharp sword you need to wield to make an adjustment, the only method leading to that round of applause, and the strategy that results in feedback, money, and admiration. Iteration is an empowering behavior—it's the most empowering behavior there is.

You're not screwed because things aren't working. You're just on the wrong path. The iteration isn't yet quite right, and often a huge departure from what you're currently doing is not required. The idea you're offering doesn't work. Should you give up? Well, maybe it needs to be priced fifty dollars less. Maybe it needs to be priced fifty dollars more. The rapid iterators are the ones who win. More to the point, as every successful start-up founder knows, it's whoever learns, fails, and learns the fastest that wins. At no point is the market ever telling you that your idea isn't any good. It's telling you it's not working because something's wrong; it's encouraging you to think and try harder.

I suppose it's possible that "they" just don't understand you. Maybe people don't appreciate what you're doing. It's more likely, though, that if you're making contact with enough people, and enough people see what you're doing, whatever it is, they're not wrong.

You are.

Once you internalize this, you can make the necessary refinements until you get it right—plain and simple. Iteration is the way of finding truth in a calm and composed manner. Think of it as the game of Hot and Cold that kids from every neighborhood from the housing projects all the way to Darien, Connecticut, play.

Here's how it goes: One kid is blindfolded and goes around the classroom looking for the key or the snow globe or whatever it is. "Cold, cold, cold," the class warns them. Then, "Warmer, warmer." And then everyone starts screaming: "Hot, hot! You're burning up now, you're on fire!" When the kid puts their hand on the object, they win the game, and then the next kid is blindfolded. It's fun. No kid ends up at the end of an empty bar drinking Michelob if he doesn't find the key—the kid always finds the damn thing eventually, and then it's someone else's turn to play.

Life is no different. Instead of sitting around and wallowing, try listening to the market and then adjust. The more time wallowing, the less progress you'll make.

Iteration is the only technique that, with ample time, will get you out of any situation. Even with limited time, it's often the only thing we've got. So learn to get comfortable with it.

Iteration means simply trying lots of different things and slowly narrowing the options to a solution. The steps could be seen as follows:

1. Cataloging various options to try
2. Grouping similar options into categories
3. Testing the first option as soon as possible

There's always a way out. In fact, there are many ways out! You just need to begin working through potential solutions.

Like a janitor with an enormous key ring, you'll find the key that fits the lock even when it's buried in the midst of hundreds of identical-looking keys. Similarly, trying the wrong key in the lock isn't a "failure," it's an iteration—just try another key.

Are you stressed? Do you need to make more money? Need to pay your rent? Do you want to marry an opera singer? Well, get iterating. Get out there and start trying other solutions. Until one works, the faster and the more solutions you try, the faster you're going to get what you want, which is money, admiration, customers, leads. At no point are you left without the behavior of iteration as long as you're standing on this earth.

Yes, some people get *lucky* on their first business. Someone created a mop that wrings itself out because she had this great idea in her kitchen. Yet there are other people—almost all the rest of us— who chisel away at a boulder. Mark Cessario, the founder of Liquid Death sparkling water (valued at over a billion dollars), said about his rapidly growing business that he never had an epiphany in the shower. No, instead he compared his experience to something more like sculpting, to chipping away at and refining a massive block of stone. So even something as cool and trendy as Liquid Death is a product of iteration, a product of testing and seeing what works and what doesn't work. I'm sure I need not point out how crowded the damn *water* business is.

REMOVE THE WORD *LUCK* FROM YOUR VOCABULARY

Let's not sit around and think, "Well, I didn't get lucky on that, I guess I'll give up." Really Rich has nothing to do with luck—let me prove it.

Luck is just *successfully reiterating and getting results earlier than you or others expect.* But society thinks, "Iterate and get results tomorrow? Luck. Iterate and get results in four months? Hard work." How is this not the same thing at play?

In this respect, luck isn't some mystical fairy dust that some have and some don't. Instead of giving up, simply consider the underwhelming state you find yourself in to be *not the right iteration.* See what you can modify.

I'll break this down further. One person iterated ten times over a year, and the next guy, a hundred times over ten years. Eventually, both got it right, and both realized the same truth about marketing their respective product. But we don't call the person who toiled for ten years lucky because it took a relatively long time for him to reach truth. So, was Thomas Edison lucky? No, he was a brilliant scientist who had the insight to develop early iterations that worked.

Naval Ravikant, whom I admire, has written extensively on luck. He categorizes it into four types—none of which, by the way, really approximates what I'm arguing in the context of becoming Really Rich. As far as I'm concerned, luck is only luck from the perspective of the recipient of the luck. Otherwise, the universe is just a soup of randomness and you happen to be the one to get it.

But that's not how business works—that's how the lottery works.

The lottery isn't itself lucky; the person who cashes in the winning numbers is lucky; everyone else is an unlucky loser. Same with casinos: for every winner there are six thousand losers clutching a warm beer over a cold hand. A casino is certainly not generating luck. Is the universe lucky, or are the people that have life the lucky ones? The universe is a jumble of data and matter and whatever else it's made of; luck is as much a real part of the universe as life is. It's defined only from the perspective of the recipient.

If you succeed in business, I guarantee that you didn't just get lucky. And anyone who thinks you did must believe that luck is the only way to get what they want out of life. Nothing can be further from the truth, and in fact that is a disempowering belief. Iteration—constant and deeply considered—is the only path to success.

The innovator who had a great idea that just didn't mature or that was framed incorrectly for the market—an idea that somebody else picked up for a song and then created something with five or ten years later—that innovator is not unlucky. Rather, he's someone who did not iterate enough.

Common knowledge for contemporary entrepreneurs is to try a lot of solutions until you find the right one. And this is absolutely correct. Meanwhile, the people who strike it rich through pure dumb luck, the ones who hit it out of the park on their first shot, aren't the magically fortunate ones. Others may view them as genius visionaries, they might be smart, they might be wise, but they are nothing more than people who iterated correctly early on.

And, by the way, such people probably don't even exist.

THE POWER OF ITERATION

Jamie Siminoff, the founder of a smart home security tech company now known as Ring, was famously and publicly turned down on *Shark Tank*, a show composed of an incredibly small number of decision-makers. What I love about Siminoff's story is that it really didn't matter whether any of those hotshot gatekeepers, from Mark Cuban to Mr. Wonderful, loved his product or not. The market adored his product—and it's the market that considered it to be valuable to the tune of a billion dollars, which is what Amazon paid Siminoff for it a short five years later.

Let's rewind a bit. A hundred years ago, back when cars were first rolling off production lines and replacing horse-and-buggy transportation, both masking tape and Scotch tape were invented by a young guy named Dick Drew, who worked for 3M. At the time, 3M solely produced sandpaper. One of the innovations in auto marketing back then was to paint new cars with attractive, two-tone designs, in contrast to the plain black models typically available. Manufacturers would glue newspaper to the chassis to try to spray-paint them, but this did not work well. Drew reported all this feedback to 3M, and for a while the company funded his attempts to create a sticky adhesive tape. The product needed hundreds of iterations—what was the right composition to make it stick, but not stick too much? What was the right paper to use so that it didn't roll back? It took him years to figure this out.

Both Siminoff and Drew, like every single successful entrepreneur, listened to their respective markets and iterated until it worked. Was Siminoff luckier than Drew because he got there faster? Of course not. If anything, he just managed to get it right in fewer tries. In fact, I'd argue that Drew made a far greater impact on the world, even though it took longer. Notably today, here's how 3M describes itself on its website:

> Our success and longevity were not apparent from the start. We tried. We failed. We tried something new. Repeat cycle. Innovation and perseverance drove our founders, and it continues to drive 3Mers today.

BELIEVE IN YOURSELF

It doesn't matter what one person says about anything. It doesn't matter what your mom and dad think. It doesn't matter what your next-door neighbor says. It doesn't matter what your best friend says. It doesn't matter what your boss thinks. *It matters what the market says.*

I'm not saying to trust your gut and stick to your guns no matter what. Whoever tells you to do that is also full of it and doesn't know what they're talking about. That's the old advice that has misled far too many into ruin. What I'm saying is *don't* stick to your guns when the entire market is telling you it doesn't want your product! Change your approach. Skip the gatekeepers and go directly to the market, and then actually listen to what it has to say. Mom and Dad are two people. In your niche market there may be hundreds or even millions.

Thanks to technological developments, you have direct access to the market faster and cheaper than ever before. Believe it when people say they don't want what you're offering. You have to trust what it means when people don't purchase your service. Sure, you might be able to say, "Well, okay, artificial intelligence will get better in the future, so I'm going to hang tight because I have a theory that this will work better in a couple months or years." That's a totally valid iteration. In contrast, the biggest tragedy is someone wasting their life on something that nobody responds to.

If Dick Drew had access to the internet in 1925, I can guarantee that the invention of Scotch tape would not have taken years. Today an entrepreneur can reach a large segment of the market almost immediately, but Drew had to hoof it to carmaker after carmaker to get some sort of a consensus on every iteration of his tape. Today, he probably could have run a Facebook ad, targeted stakeholders at automotive design shops, and obtained an answer in about forty-five minutes. What twenty years ago may have taken six months now takes a few weeks to test.

Amazingly, this phenomenon hasn't been modeled out or promoted in business training curricula, because the truth is that a person's ability to change is what dictates his or her success—more than anything else. Your emotionless, constant evolution, your focus on what's true for your product is why you're successful. No innovator *just has a knack for things.* What they have a knack for is sorting through information: Pete Townshend (the songwriter for The Who, one of the most successful rock bands of all time) famously revised The Who's classic rock opera *Tommy* to feature a Pinball Wizard instead of a "guitar wizard" after a casual comment made by a music critic over lunch. And you're sitting there worried about tweaking your "perfect" product?

Of course, it's human nature to think that trying a new solution is a setback, because it implicitly suggests that *you were wrong.* And that hurts. Okay, it even kind of sucks. But if you can get over that, if you can set aside your ego and arrogance—because that's what it is—you get smarter. You learn faster. You iterate faster. There's a reason why Rich Guy, rather than Really Rich Guy, is arrogant and pigheaded—he doesn't see a better solution because he thinks he knows best in all situations. Would you rather always be right, or would you rather be successful?

The way that I operate now is to take every new idea, examine it in an open-minded way, and then decide whether I want to develop it or say it's not for me. If it's worth considering, I raise the idea with my staff. Sometimes a colleague expresses how happy they are because I'm listening to their ideas, but my answer is, "I'm not listening to your ideas—I need your ideas!"

I'm not doing anyone a favor by listening to their ideas to make them feel heard and cozy. No, it's because without their ideas, we don't model different scenarios and try new things. To me, what a business leader does is listen, incorporate, internalize, and then make a decision. That decision might be wrong. But it's the best estimation of what to do with the new information that's just come to light.

We don't learn when we're right. We only learn when we're wrong. You should know that if you've been on a tear of right decisions, you're probably on your high horse, and you need to be careful. There are archetypal myths about this sort of thing: Icarus was sure he was right, and what ended up happening to him?

The print news media was painfully slow to adapt to the internet age, in part due to hubris. They had sold newspapers forever, and they were certain that they'd keep selling newspapers forever, but of course that wasn't necessarily true. They lost their perspective on their own product: their attitude was one of wanting people *to read the physical paper*, instead of wanting consumers *to become educated on current events*.

LOW-RISK MICRO-TESTING IDEAS

But let's return to the basics of iteration, and by this I mean the practical usefulness of a micro-test.

A micro-test, or developing an MVP (minimum viable product), is the smallest particle of your "big idea" that, if it works, suggests that the whole big thing might work too. This concept is commonplace in tech and software development but should be part of anyone's toolkit, whether they're working with woodcarving or JavaScript.

The exercise of breaking big things into smaller pieces should become so second nature that you think of the "tests" at the same time as the big picture. You'll find that no idea is too big or too terrifying with this technique.

If your dream is to open a school for young musicians, don't go immediately to rent a $10,000 per month auditorium. Rather, toss some fluorescent-colored flyers into the hallway of the nearest school and see if anyone emails you to sign up. If they do, start promoting it online.

A micro-test is both:

- rapid and
- cheap.

Notice how flyers, rather than beautiful full-color pamphlets, were tossed into the hallway. Flyers are something everyone can afford.

Many don't break ground on a grand idea because it's not easy or comfortable to shift from looking at the mountaintop to taking the first step. Hitting your big idea may require new relationships, know-how, or resources that you don't have at this present moment. That doesn't mean you can't begin to make headway with virtually *nothing*.

Even the most capital-intensive, high-risk businesses on the planet, such as rocket development and space exploration, are funded on well-developed *ideas*. It's actually so expensive to build a rocket prototype that only mental hours are expended in advance.

In fact, SpaceX was founded on an idea without proof of concept. Elon Musk presented his vision to a group of aerospace engineers and investors, many of whom were initially skeptical. But Musk was persistent and convinced them to buy in.

In 2006, SpaceX successfully launched its first rocket, the Falcon 1, into orbit. Since then, the company has continued to innovate and develop new technologies, such as the Falcon Heavy and the reusable Falcon 9 rocket. Today, SpaceX is one of the most successful and innovative space companies in the world.

Musk once said: "We're famous for turning things from impossible to *late*."

Here are a few common micro-testing strategies:

- Simple website or lead page
- Verbal or digital survey of strangers
- Low-budget search ads (Google Ads or other)
- A consortium of similar-minded people or an online community

This list is not exhaustive or prescriptive.

Collect information in the way that's most accessible and relevant to you.

DON'T STAY FOR TOO LONG IN ONE ITERATION

When you've been iterating and reinventing your product, and the market consistently fails to respond, there will come a time to consider whether you've gone as far as you can go. The key and, really, final question then becomes: Will time make this better? Is there some reason why time might help me with this challenge? If the answer is no, then you've got to stop. If the answer is maybe or yes, then by all means stick around (if you can afford to).

Those in the sneaker business in the 1960s saw gradual increases in sales, and companies such as Nike could anticipate that the product would be more and more marketable. Maybe no one expected the explosion in sneaker sales in the 1980s, but Nike certainly had banked on better days coming ahead. On the other hand, and on a more personal note, after doing everything I could to lead a New Orleans blues band, I had to reluctantly acknowledge that blues music wasn't likely to see a market resurgence before I'd be flat broke. Time wasn't on my side.

Of course, there are always unknowns in the market. Who anticipated pickleball becoming the fastest-growing sport in America? Pickleball was invented as a children's game in 1965—it took more than fifty years for its market to mature!

IT'S EMPOWERING TO UNDERSTAND THAT IN BUSINESS THERE'S NO such thing as luck because it means that anyone has the capacity to continue to iterate. There's no need to go through the day moaning and groaning, "Woe is me, I didn't get it yet." Instead, turn your idea this way or that way today. Ultimately, if you're diligent enough in your iteration, you can't not eventually hit on something satisfactory.

If anything, luck is the ability to iterate, and unluckiness is the failure to do so.

Luck is landing on a solution that's true and satisfactory early. Unluckiness is stopping on a solution that is unsatisfactory and probably too late.

If you get up every day and say, "I'm going to take another swing at it today," that's a lot more empowering than thinking you're doomed. People who work in software might understand this better than anyone, because in software iteration happens every day—you're constantly watching and then tweaking a little thing and seeing what happens. And when it clicks...*ahhhh*. This is the way the world works.

EXERCISE

Define your biggest, wildest dream without any embarrassment about its audacity.

_____

_____

_____

Ignore the gap between where you are today and the big, wild dream.

What would prove that your big idea is workable (e.g., ticket sales, downloads, course signups, social media followers, subscribers/licensees)?

_____

_____

_____

How will you test this metric with strangers at minimal or no cost (for example, through flyers, Google Ads, voluntary interviews)?

_____

_____

_____

Determine from this test whether enough people would be interested.

If your idea passes the test, build a rudimentary version of the thing.

If your idea fails the test, test it in a new way.

If it fails again, move on to a new idea.

CHAPTER 5

Treasure Your Time

APPRECIATE HOW TIME IS PRICELESS

B ENJAMIN FRANKLIN FAMOUSLY HELD THAT "TIME IS MONEY."
That made sense, I suppose, at the advent of the Industrial Revolution in the 1700s, when wages were based on hours of production. If you were lazy and didn't work hard, you starved to death. The truth, though, is that time is far more valuable than money. From the perspective of how relatively short our lives are, time is finite; money is not. That's what makes time far more valuable. Sorry, Ben.

Time is a finite playground. Relative to each of our life spans, it has a beginning, and it has an end. Unlike money, time is also the only commodity, so to speak, that, once it's gone, never comes back. This means that the more iterations you can pack into your fixed amount of time, the more likely you're going to generate an outcome to your satisfaction. Money, on the other hand, is a mere contrivance of various governments that encourages trade— and it's infinite. Need more money to finance a war? Turn on the printer.

Time is the missing link between value and its subsequent reward. Time has unlimited potential, whereas physical money can only be "turned into" goods existing today. But the truth is that many people are unable to visualize the importance of the future or conceptualize the notions of compounding interest and other critical second- and third-order magnitudes of actions taken today.

We "build tomorrow today" to the extent that profit is extracted from the future via a clear vision for offering value. The concept of liquidity, or turning one financial object into another, is critical to understanding time—the most liquid asset of all because of its sheer potential. After all, with enough time, even the universe and life on Earth came into existence.

The town of Matera, a historic village in the Basilicata region of southern Italy, offers an instructive example. Today it's known for its ancient cave dwellings, stunning architecture, and rich cultural heritage, and it's become one of Italy's most desirable tourist destinations. For centuries, the town went through cycles of war, famine, and growth, only to be conquered again and again.

As late as the 1950s, the town's residents were so poor that they withdrew to living in caves and rudimentary dwellings cut into the tuff rock, forming the historically poor district known as the Sassi. Around that time, when Italy began to rebuild following World War II, the living conditions and sanitation issues in this forgotten village were so bad that the Italian government formally declared the Sassi to be an "area of national shame." Plans were made to evacuate the residents and demolish the entire district. However, a few policymakers and activists saw things differently, and in the 1980s Matera underwent a process of revitalization. By 1993, it was declared a UNESCO World Heritage Site, which drew the first tourists to the area.

This designation raised the appeal of the area—the ruined caves, once disgusting hovels of poverty, were now of cultural and historic interest. As tourists began to explore the area, investment dollars followed. Hotels were developed, pizza places opened, Matera was used as a backdrop in numerous films, including the James Bond movie *No Time to Die*, and the residents of Matera suddenly found themselves in a booming economy. Their town had been rebranded as stylish almost overnight. For them, the future became better and richer, although I'm sure, after years of sheltering in a dilapidated cave exposed to harsh elements, it must have been tempting to think the future promised otherwise.

In the context of markets, time allows for the expression of value: the more time you have, the greater the opportunity that consumers in the market can "vote," meaning express their collective opinion, about what you're offering. In this view, the more time you have, the greater your potential for opportunity.

Historically, humanity has assigned immense importance not so much directly to wealth but to time management. After all—and we can go back to the development of the wheel for this—the effect of technological advancement is always time reduction. And as a core tenet of the Really Rich approach makes clear, the value provided by technological development can be boiled down to whether it makes things easier. The wheel meant that people, dead wildebeests, or boulders, or whatever our ancestors needed to move, could be transported faster. The printing press allowed for the rapid production and dissemination of books, which precipitated the Renaissance. The steam engine powered the Industrial Revolution and led to faster transportation, manufacturing, and industry. The telegraph and telephone gave birth to rapid, global communications. The harnessing of electricity might have killed the kerosene industry, not to mention whaling (whale blubber once fueled lamps), but it more importantly led to the development of innumerable innovations that made life easier. The internal combustion engine and the advent of airplanes revolutionized transportation, making it faster. And the computer and internet, of course, transformed the way we all do business and produced the digital age. All of this underscores the supreme value civilization places on time.

Technology compresses time, meaning that we have the ability to impact people in shorter increments of time, which gives us more opportunities to continue to make an impact—in other words, to iterate. Put it this way: Would you rather have infinite time or infinite money? Obviously, infinite time would allow you to make infinite money, but not the other way around. It's why vampires in fantasy novels are so rich—they've lived forever, learned, and acted accordingly! In a sense, vampires enjoy the luxury of futurecasting.

FUTURECASTING

Futurecasting is a strategic planning and forecasting technique that involves envisioning and anticipating possible future scenarios and trends in order to make informed decisions and plan for the future. It's a proactive approach individuals, businesses, and organizations use to better prepare for various possibilities and uncertainties.

Put another way, futurecasting is the act of creating a vivid description of where you'd like to head without having the faintest idea of how you'll get there. The "how" isn't important right now. With a preliminary idea of who you are, from exploration of your childhood interests or other exercises in the previous chapters, you're ready to create your ideal destination—nothing will motivate you more out of this dark corner of the woods than a tasty fruit garden on the other side.

Futurecasting can be accomplished in two ways:

1. With closed eyes in a relaxed, meditative state
2. With pen and paper

The idea here is to pick a single moment and build it in your mind's eye (or on paper) as richly as possible.

- What is your dream moment?
- How do you feel in this desired moment?
- How do others regard you?
- How do you look?

It's helpful to return to this vision over time so it increases in resolution and emotional intensity. Don't be afraid to mold and refine this vision as you try new things and previous desires are experienced as disappointing.

By the high-fidelity nature of your future cast, you'll know which paths could potentially get you there and which wouldn't.

In other words, if you love taking a daily swim, ensure that you're positioning yourself close to the sea or a swimming pool rather than as a flight attendant.

Futurecasting—or what I also call time filtering—will provide more information for your journey than anything you could see in the present physical world of tangled branches in front of you.

TIME FILTERING

Because time is your one truly finite resource, spend it wisely. Not only is it a limited resource, but there's also an opportunity cost, of sorts, to the extent you spend each moment on a specific activity. Inherently, this means you're sacrificing the opportunity to engage in another act. Your choices matter, making it essential to prioritize and organize yourself. Moreover, as discussed fully in the next chapter, knowing your desired quality of life is essential for making decisions about time. For the Really Rich, life is not only about wealth generation—our days also include personal relationships, health, and for most people, artistic pursuits. You might find you have only five hours a day to devote to business because you've also chosen to coach your kids and any other number of things that interest you and add to your quality of life.

How, then, do you turn those five hours into the outcome that you require? Do you need human assistance or AI support? Do you need a virtual assistant from overseas that you can afford? What you don't want to do is let this precious, finite measure of time slip through your fingers like sand. Why do some people have wild success compared to others with respect to time filtering? To a person, the successful ones are managing to apply as much of their time toward iteration as they can right now, given their circumstances.

The drill is to trim the fat from your time. I'm not suggesting that every waking moment of your day has to be applied toward iteration. But a significant portion of it does, and the rest of it should be spent in ways that you find are rewarding.

As the thought experiment goes, if with infinite time you set a monkey to tap away at a typewriter, it'll eventually, money-back guaranteed, write *The Great Gatsby*. If it doesn't have infinite time, of course, the chance of that happening is a lot lower. But we're not monkeys, nor are we iterating purely at random, so we have the ability to recognize that time is our most limited resource and then train ourselves to maximize it.

What we need to do with our time, of course, is to hone our respective crafts. We get smarter and better and we iterate our product or service. As the market continues to offer feedback, we grow more comfortable with what we're doing, and repeated iterations drive our abilities to adapt.

Jeff Bezos is a prime example of maximizing time. He's famously disciplined about it, publicly revealing that he doesn't take meetings before 10:00 a.m. and won't make substantive decisions after 3:00 p.m. He's recognized that he's most productive between ten and three, and this is of utter importance to him. And who could argue that Amazon is in any way stymied by this approach?

I'm not even remotely suggesting that you should work only from ten to three; as for myself, I choose to put in more like twelve- to fourteen-hour workdays. The point is that time management has to be to your satisfaction—not to either my or Jeff Bezos's satisfaction. If you're sitting there wanting more out of life, then it's up to you to sort that out. And if you're comfortable sitting on the couch and everything's good, and you've got a little business humming in the background, who am I to tell you to go build a Fortune 500 company? Every element of becoming Really Rich is applied to *your* road map, *your* futurecasting, and *your* unique disposition.

But do ask yourself honestly if you're where you want to be right now.

THE WHY

What's your motivation when it comes to generating an income? Some people future cast to work hard through their thirties and maybe forties to earn enough to then sit back and enjoy resting and traveling the rest of their lives. In other words, they work extremely hard now to enjoy leisure time later.

Being Really Rich, though, isn't necessarily about the myth of grinding. Yes, we need to recognize how much of a finite resource we all have with respect to time, but we're also not going to stop iterating just because we've turned sixty or seventy.

If we're talking about financial success, the Really Rich formula is to iterate until you hit a point when you're monetarily satisfied—however you define that. But there's more to this. We're not fighting for financial success with the hope of simply relaxing in twenty far-off years. The key reflection, instead, is to determine whether you enjoy what you're doing right now.

I marvel at old friends or associates who slave away at salaried jobs they hate, squirreling away money to retire sometime in their mid-sixties to a boat docked on a peaceful lake in Arizona or a cove in Florida. None of us really know what the future has in store. You may not have good health in your sixties, you may have become bitter from decades of unhappiness at your workplace, or you might end up not saving enough for the cost of your dream decades in the future. Heck, Arizona may not even have many lakes left in thirty years!

The Really Rich live in the moment. They find satisfying work by knowing what they're good at and iterating until the market sees value in it. You can't really defer enjoyment until later, because the truth is, with that attitude, you'll never get there. The habit of suffering over a long period of time is, well, a hard habit to break.

I occasionally wonder what life might be like for me in twenty-five years, but I don't dwell on it. I'm much more concerned about what I'm doing today or tomorrow: How are today and tomorrow going to be as fun and satisfying as they can be? In this respect, I future cast my business or professional life, but not the elements of life that satisfy my soul. I can tell you that a two-dollar espresso tastes just as good when I had $1,000 in my bank account as it does when I now have far more.

I once had lunch with a fairly successful lawyer who remarked about his business, "Well, if everything fails, I'll just move down to Mexico and start selling fishing tours." And he was serious about this—he really dreamed about taking tourists out to fish in the Gulf of Mexico. In other words, he needs his whole life to *fail* in order to pursue his *dream*. That's how disconnected he was from his dream. Somehow this insane logic was the only glue that held his reality together for why he *wasn't* trolling for mackerel. He's a lawyer over here, and then there's this vision of captaining deep-sea fishing tours somewhere over there. They don't intersect and never will. It's like playing a game of catch with both hands tied behind your back and blaming your buddy for throwing a slider. That's not being Really Rich.

Are you doing what you're doing because you love it? Or are you doing what you're doing as an expedient means, and not really loving it, because someone told you it would be a good, safe, or practical choice? If you're living life this latter way, I'm afraid I have some painful news for you: you're heading in the wrong direction, and your two roads—your reality and your dream—will continue to diverge as finite time slips away. Marriage, children, health challenges, and all other practical aspects of life will intrude on your path, themselves demanding more time, more money, and more of you. If there's no escape today, there's no escape tomorrow.

Again, it all comes back to what's satisfying to you. I have another friend, an older finance guy, who devoted thirty years to developing a successful hedge fund business with which he made a killing. And in his early fifties he stepped away, financially secure, to devote himself to painting in his living room. He's become a relatively successful artist ten years later—not Basquiat level, but successful enough to get critical notice and significant gallery sales. Admittedly, this was a dream he'd had all along—he loved what he did at his hedge fund, and he was known for his creative strategies there, but in his heart he wanted to paint without any concerns about his financial stability.

The difference between the painter and the lawyer is that the painter had a futurecasting strategy, and he engaged in a financial profession that he enjoyed and that allowed him to manifest his dream, which he knew full well would never support him financially; the lawyer has nothing more than a dream that will slowly erode his quality of life and sense of humanity.

GETTING WHAT YOU WANT

Warren Buffett correctly observed that you can have anything you want, but not *everything* you want. Another way to look at this from the Really Rich perspective is that you can have anything you want, but *you don't get to decide what it is that gets you there*—the market will tell you. You're entitled to your desired state of life, but you don't know exactly what's going to get you there or how it's going to look. Neither will you know how long it's going to take. Think of time as a river and iteration as the boat you're on that will eventually allow you to reach your destination. It may take a few months; it may take a few years.

Inevitably, there will be rocky stretches and fast currents along the way. Even now, as I'm engaged in the development of new AI products that, once they hit, could dwarf any of my past earnings, there are times when I need to generate greater liquidity or infusions of capital because the products require more testing and iteration and expensive man-hours. This is the entrepreneurial dance I engage in weekly.

So I may, from time to time, have to generate additional funding with other less exciting businesses that I have, such as consulting. This is a choice I make. And I don't hate consulting—in fact, it's stimulating because it demands creative energy. But, in a sense, as a consultant, I'm working for others rather than solely building something for myself. Now that, I don't love. Truthfully, the only thing standing between me and the generation of some extra capital is my ego and the related resistance to doing something other than my Rich vs. Really Rich video series and my insurance start-up, Revise Annuity.

We all experience this push and pull between fighting for our dreams and having to also do what's practical. The idea of an entrepreneur doing what they're good at, or doing what they like, is naturally tempered by circumstances at times. There is a spectrum of things that you're willing to do and not willing to do, given the circumstances you find yourself in. This back-and-forth is part of our journey as we iterate down the currents of time. Consulting, in my case, is something like an expedient means.

All the practical and expedient means available won't be pretty. If we zoom back to my time in New Orleans after my band broke up, my means was working in a clothing store for fourteen dollars an hour. I had to work there because at the time it was the only thing between me sleeping in a bed and me getting evicted. Certainly, my game plan was never, ever under any circumstances to remain in that clothing store for long. It took a full six months to escape with my first business and my life as I know it today.

Now, there's a difference between accommodating your circumstances on the journey toward your goal and completely compromising yourself by doing something that you know you don't love doing. As for me, if Goldman Sachs were to call me and ask me to join their wealth management team—the sort of well-paying job that I did in my years after college—and they offered to pay me a million bucks to do it, my answer would be an unshakable no. Of course, I'd love the million dollars—who wouldn't?—but not at the cost of derailing my journey toward doing what I truly know I love to do. Oddly, working at a clothing store for crappy wages was more on the path toward freedom for me than going back to a shiny finance job would have been.

All this is a matter of ends versus means. If you compromise your dream (the end), you've conceded the ability to reach for a Really Rich life. You're not going to get the thing that you want. Be very cautious about taking this path. But if you indulge in a meaningful endeavor (the means) that helps you reach your dream (the end), you're still on your Really Rich journey. And it doesn't matter if anyone else on the outside sees this, as long as you do.

Some people have a subconscious fear of succeeding, or they don't fully believe in their own innate abilities to carve their unique path. I can't tell you how many friends I've had who go to law school because they're intelligent and don't really know what else to do. Some have a vague idea about working in corporate law for a year or two and then jumping over to something like the entertainment industry—and that's a superb plan, if that's indeed their dream and they're determined to execute it. But most don't do this. Most graduate law school and find themselves on a partner track at their respective firms—and only a small percentage of them will actually achieve partner. They're playing a trick on themselves.

Here's a secret: the ones who make it to partner are the ones who *really want to be* a partner at a law firm; the ones who don't are the ones with a secret ambition to actually work at something else. But after eight, ten, twelve years of trying to make partner, that original dream, which wasn't burning too brightly to begin with, has been snuffed out by their own selves. And unless they iterate their way out of this, they're looking into the future from the perspective of a job they hate. I'm not picking on lawyers—the same can be said for the majority of business graduates as well as those who take positions at banks, finance companies, and the like. This isn't some rare case; rather, most people I interact with find themselves in this conundrum. Perhaps you're dealing with a similar situation right now?

For some reason, and for some people, the fear of succeeding is as scary as the fear of failing! I'm convinced my New Orleans band started to break up, at least in part, because we had reached a crossroads where the effort was actually working—we were performing at the best clubs and were on the verge of what looked at the time to be a major record deal. Were we going to be famous? Well, for some people in the band, that was scary as hell, especially the ones who didn't want to be famous in the first place. So maybe someone starts drinking again. Maybe another starts doing drugs or another stops showing up to practice. And it ends there. It did for my band and my dreams of getting on the cover of *Rolling Stone*.

There's a famous slogan that was created for the first Earth Day, in 1970, that goes: "We have met the enemy, and he is us." If there's a voice inside suggesting you can't reach your dream, that you can't do what you love—whether it's from your parents, the media, your teachers, or just "common wisdom" floating in the ether—I'm here to tell you that you can. Iteration is your secret sauce, and unless you're very, very old, time is still on your side.

It's okay to bob and weave as you make your way toward becoming the Really Rich you; it's not okay to relegate your dream to a far-off future that you're not likely to reach because you stopped working toward it. In fact, bobbing and weaving is core to any major success story.

It's okay to compromise using an expedient means; it's not okay to surrender to what someone else thinks you should do or be.

Keep your eye on *your* prize. At some point before he was BRAD PITT, in neon lights, Brad Pitt was waiting tables and working odd jobs to get by. Nowhere in this set of Really Rich behaviors is there an instruction to stomp your feet and demand that you receive something *now*. No, first you have to hone your idea, get market feedback, and iterate and iterate again—often for years. A young Brad Pitt painted houses not because he wanted to be a house painter but because it was the means for him to pay for acting lessons to perfect his craft, learn who he was and would be as an actor, find someone to give him a chance, and then nail down the right role. But I doubt he would have been a house painter forever. My hunch, instead, is that this theoretical Brad Pitt who didn't make it as an actor would have found himself in some other performative profession.

Consider this perspective from *Game of Thrones* star Peter Din-klage, who comparatively trod an even tougher road: "I hate that word—'lucky.' It cheapens a lot of hard work. Living in Brooklyn in an apartment without any heat and paying for dinner at the bodega with dimes, I don't think I felt myself lucky back then. Doing plays for fifty bucks and trying to be true to myself as an artist and turn-ing down commercials where they wanted a leprechaun. Saying I was lucky negates the hard work I put in and spits on that guy who's freezing his ass off back in Brooklyn."[1] Dinklage understands per-haps more than anyone that "luck," as we've been told in the game of hitting it big, is a fabulous lie.

I don't know if time is relative to space or whether mass and energy can affect the flow of time—those answers would be found in one of Einstein's books. And I don't really care whether time is an objective or subjective experience or somehow an illusion. I do know that we must appreciate time as priceless because our lives are finite, and of all the Really Rich resources, time is the only finite one.

Use it wisely and iterate efficiently before your dream, whatever it may be, slips away. And because we're all interconnected in one way or another, I'd be worse off for it too. Don't you dare withhold your gifts and talents from the world that I inhabit alongside you.

EXERCISE

What are the things you do (or have to do) daily that irritate or tire you?

_____

_____

_____

How can you decrease or replace these tasks within your current means?

_____

_____

_____

Envision what it will take to remove any of these tasks entirely in the future:

_____

_____

_____

Brainstorm five ways that can lead you to never having to perform these tasks again. Write them down:

_____

_____

_____

_____

_____

Review this list and isolate the easiest path forward.

CHAPTER 6

Reset Your Focus

OPTIMIZE FOR QUALITY OF LIFE, NOT A DOLLAR AMOUNT

In 2002, a bespectacled and charming West Virginia construction executive in a black cowboy hat named Jack Whittaker won a $314 million Powerball jackpot, which, at the time, was the biggest lottery prize in history. Whittaker was known as a generous guy, and he enjoyed his newfound ability to provide gifts to friends and people in need—including, reportedly, the local church, waitresses he'd meet at diners, and, of course, local strippers. That is, until he had no money left. Perhaps too trusting in nature, Whittaker lost a great deal of his fortune as a result of scams, scandals, lawsuits, and other personal setbacks.

Within fifteen years of his windfall, his wife had left him, his house had burned down, he ran afoul of the law, and he lost children and grandchildren to poor health and drugs. Before he passed away in 2020, Whittaker said he wished "he had just torn up the ticket."[1]

Whittaker's story fascinates me. Not surprisingly, he's not the only one this type of thing happened to. Plenty of lottery winners lost it all.

Lara and Roger Griffiths's marriage ended in divorce less than a decade after the British couple won a $2.19 million jackpot—that's a whole lot less than the three hundred or so million Whittaker squandered. Roger chased his rock star dreams and spent big bucks for his band to release an album (I can relate). Lara got a taste for the high life and the couple bought exotic cars, an expensive house, designer clothes and accessories, and a pricey private school education for their daughter. They dumped hundreds of thousands of dollars into opening a salon, where Lara later worked as an employee to make ends meet. In the end, the couple reportedly was left with less than ten dollars.[2] Clearly, lotto money doesn't come along with the lessons on how to make more of it or even keep some of it for long.

The acquisition of money (especially lots of it) without a proper understanding of the role money plays in one's quality of life will ruin you.

Five years after Kentucky resident David Lee Edwards won a $27 million jackpot, he was penniless and living in a storage shed with his wife.[3] The couple had squandered their fortune on the typical goodies that sink so many lucky winners: they bought dozens of high-end cars, mansions, and a plane. They blew through $3 million in the first three months—even by my standards that's pretty fast. By the end of the first year, $12 million was gone. Soon after, the couple had spiraled into drug addiction, and just twelve years after the win changed the course of his life, David Lee Edwards died alone and broke in hospice care at the age of fifty-eight. What could be more horrifying than this tale?

I'm the last one to argue that money is the root of all evil, or that money somehow leads to unhappiness. I am certain, though, that money without consideration for quality of life can be easily lost.

Money itself is a neutral thing—it's like electricity, which of course can be used to both illuminate and destroy, depending on the intent of whoever's wielding it. It can light your house and keep you warm, or it can be applied to electrocute someone to death.

Many have made the mistake, including this author, of not only frittering away funds but also seeking arbitrary dollar-amount goals and ignoring any and all details that get in the way. The single-mindedness of a financial goal causes it to be highly attainable, often well before the seeker can believe it. However, in the achievement of the riches many, like these poor lottery "winners," find themselves disappointed or downright depressed. This is due to two errors of judgment: misunderstanding what money is and underestimating the importance of key lifestyle factors.

Having not taken into consideration critical factors such as health, free time, or quality of work interactions, we end up achieving a goal that is worthless. This is called "having all the money in the world and no time to spend it," a common label for those in the investment banking industry, which welcomes thousands of new recruits every year. Toiling for upward of seventy or more hours per week, recent grads find themselves with plenty of money but an extremely low quality of life.

This is all because we tend not to consider how it is we want to live, quite apart from how much we want to make. When a quality of life is defined in detailed terms, however, we find that many attractive paths to wealth actually become disqualified, while many new paths are illuminated in the process. For example, someone seeking the great outdoors and adventure shouldn't consider a career in accounting. Simple in theory, but surprisingly difficult in practice.

WHAT IS QUALITY OF LIFE?

The basic elements of any quality-of-life analysis start with health: good physical and mental health is a fundamental aspect of a satisfying existence. Access to healthcare services and a healthy lifestyle are critical. Social relationships are also important, because loneliness and social isolation can negatively impact our ability to execute other Really Rich behaviors. We also need to feel safe and secure, and we have to try to preserve our autonomy and the ability to make personal choices. If your creativity is suppressed, your humanity already has been stunted. How in the world can you then make anyone else's life easier if you're not able to think for yourself?

Curiously, optimizing for quality of life is both a goal and the only means by which we can actually achieve the target of becoming Really Rich. You can be rich, but you can't be Really Rich without tending to the rest of your life. In a sense, this is a quantitative and qualitative analysis. It's asking both how much money do you need and what will your life look like? In this scenario, one could certainly have all the money in the world while suffering with the worst quality of life. Do you want to be like old, very wealthy Howard Hughes, sitting in filth and in desperate need of a manicure? That's not an ideal state. Many of us think that having less money will lead to more personal freedom, but that's not always true either, and it's not an ideal state in any event.

It's got to be a mix of work and "extra-work" endeavors, and it's something that, again, is unique to each individual based on their disposition, interests, and goals. As with other Really Rich behaviors, the key is in defining *what's important to you specifically*, as opposed to an expectation handed down from whomever or whatever has influenced you. One size never fits all in a Really Rich analysis. Who am I to tell you how to enjoy your precious time?

Your quality of life isn't related to only nonwork activities. Let's be clear—the *quality of your work life* is a huge part of your analysis. Who do you speak to on a daily basis? Who are you interacting with? Do you have enough time with your kids and family? Are your work objectives challenging or boring? Ultimately, we want to reach a place at work where, as we've all heard certain people say, *it doesn't even feel like a job.*

Doing what you love to do is what freedom tastes like, and it is where the Really Rich reside.

ITERATION CAN BE A SLIDING SCALE

Now, all of this, of course, is a highly individualized sliding scale. I think of it as a risk–safety scale. If there are two people who long for a life in the woods, one might quit her corporate job and move to Maine, while the other enjoys the benefits of a corporate job and finds the right balance in spending a few weekends away in the woods. I have a friend who's a longtime attorney at a large corporate law firm but a poet at heart. He enjoys the perks of a relatively high salary and financial security, so he's managed to maintain a law career while also publishing several books of poetry. He knows he's not going to make a living writing poetry, or at least not at the level of income he wants, but he also recognizes what his true passion is: he's found a way, for him, to make both work. He's optimized his quality of life. He's struck a deal that's satisfying.

The paralegal who stares at the clock all day and bolts from the office at five o'clock is something like 100 percent on the side of safety on the risk–safety scale: he hates his job and counts down the minutes until he can do something he'd much rather do, whether it be perfecting his tennis game or tweaking a novel he's been working on for ten years. Another paralegal—someone who has a real interest in law and what law firms do but who chooses not to go to law school because what she really wants is enough of a salary to pursue her dream of building a thriving custom-made jewelry business— is more like at the fifty-fifty mark on the scale because she spends all of her time engaged in something she enjoys. Sure, she'd rather manage her Etsy store all day long, but for now this risk/safety ratio is working. She's optimizing her quality of life, while the first paralegal isn't.

The sign that tells you where you sit on this scale is obvious: the second you recognize that you hate your safe job is when you know that your life is misplaced. Unless you truly long for a life of no risk, which doesn't exist, you've got to reassess how you allocate your time. I'm not blaming anyone for *not* recognizing this straightaway—it's not like anyone explains any of this in school. But if you're spending 100 percent of your time in riskless, salaried work—to the exclusion of any other dream—perhaps you need a swift kick of uncertainty.

Yet everything on this spectrum is subjective. My scale or spectrum does not look like yours. A lot of what goes into what works for you is grounded in emotions and temperament. How much risk are you willing to take? It could be less than I am, it could be more. From this perspective, then, optimizing for quality of life becomes yet another exercise in iteration. Don't just sit there, but instead find out what works for you.

I have a childhood friend who hated school. Although he managed to graduate high school and even enrolled in a decent college, he had no patience to sit through lectures he thought were irrelevant to his life and dropped out after freshman year. At the age of nineteen, he took a test to become licensed as a pension fund manager, and he's worked for the past twenty years at a few different nonprofit corporations, helping to manage their pensions. At the same time, he began, back when he was nineteen, to invest money he had saved for tuition into a mix of stocks, and he became quite good at playing the market. His portfolio, which he's since diversified into fun and now valuable collectibles such as old comic books and baseball cards, is already worth a few million. So he's well on his way to becoming set financially, yet he continues to work his nine-to-five job primarily for the excellent health insurance benefits his employer offers.

Is my school friend Really Rich? To be honest, I don't know. I haven't heard him complain much about what I suppose might be a relatively boring job to which he devotes close to fifty hours a week, including the commute, but I know he spends freely on nice vacations and the best sports events and concerts. The point is, who am I, or any of us, to say? If he thinks, "I can't believe I spent twenty years doing this crap," then he's not Really Rich. If he doesn't feel that way at all, then perhaps indeed he is. The analysis, again, is what works for him. So, I beg, what works for you?

Deep down, most people don't want money. They want a particular condition of life, a state of life unique to them. Yes, it may have a loose correlation to a dollar amount—that boat you want to sail isn't cheap. Still, when people close their eyes and think about their dream, they're thinking about a state of being, a quality of life: friends and family around, fresh fruit on the table, the ability to take a vacation, the mountain retreat they once rented that they someday want to own or live in. What they're not seeing is an accountant in the background saying, "That costs $10,000, and this costs $15,000," and so forth.

Hey, wake up—do you want this life? Okay, then let's figure out how to get it. As we now know, one of the keys for living a Really Rich life is to both create your job and follow your dream. If you need to maintain your corporate job while you develop your passion, consider it a hedge and work your way toward your right balance.

You have the ability to change.

Be truthful with yourself.

Iteration + Awareness = Wealth.

WHAT MAKES WORK FULFILLING?

A recent, post-COVID Gallup poll established that only 33 percent of the entire North American workforce "feels engaged" at work. This number is even lower, 21 percent, for the rest of the world. How is this not a gigantic social crisis? This means that three out of every ten people are phoning it in at work, wishing they could do something else! And this sucks for the businesses too. Companies with highly engaged employees are 22 percent more profitable, and they enjoy much higher employee retention rates. Meanwhile, very interestingly, 40 percent of those working remotely consider themselves engaged. Perhaps they have closer contact with their "real dream" than those in the office. The entire model of corporate business in America is changing.[4]

There is, as we know, a reluctance to return to the office and an acknowledgment that many people can get the job done from home, sometimes with a higher level of efficiency. The rise of technological developments such as Zoom and Google Meet dovetailing with the sudden taste for working from home that was compelled by the national COVID lockdowns has created a new work paradigm. People like not having to commute for an hour on a crowded train with dirty vinyl seats, essentially wasting their precious time in a productivity dead zone. Who knew? And many now refuse to commute altogether. I refuse to do *anything* routinely that's outside a fifteen-minute walk from my home. I carefully plot out a gym, office, coffee shop, and neighborhood restaurants in advance of choosing a home. Setting aside the significant costs of commuting, such as car payments, insurance, gas, and commuter fares, consider how valuable that hour's commute each way is to you in terms of productive work.

Years ago, I certainly got very little accomplished on my daily commute from my home in Manhattan to a trading floor in Stamford, Connecticut. At one point, after about six months, I refused to do it any longer, and I just didn't show up to work. I couldn't commute every day anymore—I was wasting so much time that I felt I was going out of my mind. I don't recommend being as brave (read: stupid) as I was and just not showing up, but my actions, and a few days of negotiation, led to a local desk being built for me in New York a stone's throw from my apartment. (As a side note, I apologize to everyone then involved.)

Some studies have even shown that people would take as much as a $30,000 annual pay cut just to save on having to commute. That's how much commuting crushes your soul! "Take my Rolex as long as I don't have to board this train again for the rest of the year."

What are you aiming for in terms of work life? What are the elements that will lead you to enjoy your job? And do you have all this where you currently find yourself?

For me, it boils down to meaningful work, cool people, and interesting challenges. I like juggling a hundred different things at once.

And I want to earn money. Lots of it.

Outside of the office, my quality-of-life demands include health, the freedom to work out every day at a gym, a comfortable living space, and the acquisition of incredibly fast cars. I'm not immune to spending on crazy stuff.

This is a simplification, of course, because our demands and desires are multifaceted, often subtle, and constantly in flux.

When the Rich vs. Really Rich series started to hit, and my earnings were rolling in, I immediately engaged in futurecasting. I asked myself, "Now that I'm making as much as I had dreamed of earning and loving every moment of what I'm doing, what do I want my life to look like?" This may seem funny or cliché, but I would have a vision of myself, almost as if in a movie, where I'd slide out of a Ferrari with a beautiful woman and walk into a chic restaurant in Miami (where I was then living) and everyone would acknowledge me, tipping their heads as if I was a revered local hero. It seems ridiculous at first, but as my business continued to develop, and as I nurtured the courage to actualize this vision, it all actually became true. Except I started with a Porsche instead.

Of course, that was just my vision. Each of you has your very own, and mine probably isn't right for you. Moreover, my vision evolves all the time as recognition becomes less important than impact.

I've worked with a couple of brilliant AI developers, both in their mid-twenties, two dudes who are not quite there but getting closer to the verge of success. One day I was curious and casually asked them about their futurecasting, specifically about what they want in the way of quality of life. This is what they said: "We don't want normal social lives. We're so jazzed by what we do that we just want to do this shit all day long. We don't need to go to bars and party all night." With this mindset, do you think these guys have any chance of *not* succeeding?

That's their vision right now, and their company is steadily growing. Will it be their vision when they are in their forties and fifties? It might be, but then again it might not. One of them continued: "I don't even date. What a waste of time, it's so stupid. We just wanna make a lot of money. Once in a blue moon, we throw a house party, but we end up talking through our business and development challenges." And his partner laughed. "I'm sure our friends hate us."

So these are two young people living life on their own terms. Who am I to say that they're working too much? They love their lives. And I get it—you almost have to be an entrepreneur yourself to grasp the sort of flow these guys are in, the rush that's generated every hour in their day. The risks they're taking are huge, and they love it. Compared to them, I was nowhere near as savvy when I was twenty-five.

But are they Really Rich? Well, they're living the lives they chose, and they're suffering through their failures, but they're willing to suffer. Each of them could easily be making a million a year at a place like Google as a senior engineer, but instead they're making far less now but pursuing their mutual dream. I expect them to out-earn any salaried engineer in town within five years.

Although these partners are probably working sixteen-hour days, seven days a week, this is what they love and it's what they want to do. They're getting enough sleep. They're eating. They're finding ways to exercise. So they're living a Really Rich life that is as valid as another person's, someone who's crafted an eight-hour workday and spends evenings with her family and two hours at the gym. It is life on their own terms, which is what quality of life means at the end of the day.

To be Really Rich is to have a clarity of vision and to command your own destiny.

> **Rich:** What's everyone else doing?
>
> **Really Rich:** What do I want to do?

DO I NEED TO START MY OWN COMPANY?

It's important to note that a Really Rich life isn't necessarily entrepreneurial. I wrote earlier about doctors or teachers who are following their passions. Now, a teacher, in his or her futurecasting, may not have prioritized making millions of dollars. And of course that's fine: the happiest I've ever seen a teacher is when one of their students succeeds. Obviously, this, too, is a Really Rich life.

Moreover, not everyone has a pioneering type of personality. There are plenty of people who love their jobs, whether in a bank, a real estate company, or whatever it is. Are you one of these people? If not, then I suggest you find out soon what sort of work it is that will make you happy. Because if you don't imagine that, if you don't find the courage to seize it, I'm afraid that you're very unlikely to reach what it is that you truly want to do in your limited time.

The whole deal is that if you want to extract maximum value out of the game, you need to own it. And for most of us, entrepreneurship is the answer. I would say the reason for this is that humans inherently crave ownership. Or, to put it another way, from a free-will perspective, we long for the agency to do what we want to do.

The only litmus test is whether you're comfortable with your current path.

I'm not talking about a lifestyle where you sit in your bedroom and play single-player video games all day and night while Mom slips dinner under your door like you're a prisoner of your own making. You might be comfortable doing that, you might even love it, but you're not living a Really Rich life. First of all, you're not creating value for anyone else, and you're not making anyone's life easier. Second, you're not interacting with others. All this has to be part of your Really Rich futurecasting analysis.

In the early 2000s, the inventor Dean Kamen developed the Segway Personal Transporter (the Segway PT), a two-wheeled, self-balancing electric scooter that was supposed to revolutionize personal transportation by providing a clean and efficient alternative to cars for short-distance travel.

However, the development of the Segway was shrouded in secrecy, with Kamen aiming for a big reveal. Prior to its launch, the venture capitalist John Doerr speculated that it would be more important than the internet. Steve Jobs was quoted as saying that it was "as big a deal as the PC." But because Kamen kept his development of the Segway under tight wraps, working in isolation without seeking input from potential users, city planners, or other stakeholders, he subjected the product to only very limited testing with targeted base users. Accordingly, his team had a narrow understanding of how the public would perceive and use the Segway. As it turned out, he failed to anticipate challenges in integrating the device into existing transportation systems, and its high price point ended up making it less accessible to a broad market. Eventually, Jobs himself said that the Segway PT "sucked," and the media jumped on notable accidents with it involving George W. Bush, the track star Usain Bolt, and Ellen DeGeneres, among others. What a disaster!

Although the Segway did find limited niche applications in certain industries, other electric scooters went on to become much more popular in the security and tourism industries. This is a cautionary tale about the potential pitfalls of developing a product in isolation, without actively seeking and incorporating market feedback throughout the development process.

BEING CREATIVE ALL ON YOUR OWN ISN'T NECESSARILY CREATING value. Sitting in your room and painting or, in Kamen's case, inventing something that few people end up caring about isn't making anyone's life easier. In contrast, sitting in your room and iterating—in other words, continuing to paint or invent until the market recognizes and appreciates you because it loves your art or your product—that's creating value. It's not cool to work your life on a stealth mission, like Kamen's, that only you think is life-changing—the rest of the world's opinion gets to decide on that.

I would even argue that the demands of the market compel you into a more creative state. There's no growth for the painter who creates banal canvases over and over again. But for the painter who longs for accolades, there's a very powerful motivation to iterate, to perfect their craft, until the market recognizes him or her as a master. The same applies to any endeavor—from the arts to business.

WELCOMING SETBACKS

It's going to be a winding road for most of us. There will be small successes and there will also be setbacks. But if your vision is clear, then everything you do will point in one direction.

Part of this vision is to continue to be aware, as lotto winner Jack Whittaker apparently realized too late, that money alone will never equal happiness. You can't turn money into a more loving relationship with your wife, though some try to do just that. You can't spend money to achieve a healthy relationship with your kids, no matter what car you buy them for high school graduation. And you can't turn money into a peaceful night's sleep. You need to consider your quality of life, not only because it's an essential behavior utilized to earn money but also because money itself has limitations. It can't reverse time. It can only be turned into external things.

The Really Rich question is, What, for you, is the correct balance? There's no sense worrying about a loving family if you don't have enough money to turn on the lights. There are things that money can resolve and things that money can't solve—a lot of people are mixed up about what's what.

My inbox is filled with emails from younger people just starting their careers who are looking for advice. Most messages begin like this: "I don't know what I want…" Or, "I think I know what I want, but I don't know how to take the first step." What I want to respond with may seem callous, but it's true: "How the hell should I know?" It's like they're asking me to tell them what their favorite pasta dish is without ever having dined with them.

A lot of the time, however, people who know they aren't happy with their work hesitate to change careers because they confuse what I would call *imagined* constraints with real constraints. An attorney I know tells an amusing story about leaving a big corporate law firm to change careers after several years as an associate. In making her rounds from office to office to say goodbye, it occurred to her that her peers' response to her news was a mix of happiness and longing—a feeling of *I wish I could do that too*, as if they were all in prison rather than sitting in $2,000 Herman Miller office chairs and eating gourmet takeaway salads at lunch.

Of course, they weren't in prison—they were practicing law and among the highest-paid workers in the country. Yes, their real constraints may have included an inability to maintain their income and lifestyle with another endeavor but also, maybe, a misbelief that they weren't capable of doing anything other than practicing law.

But this misbelief, though real to them, is an imagined constraint. Everyone has certain unique talents and capabilities that they can exploit and that the market would welcome. If working as an associate at a large corporate law firm is your dream, then you wouldn't have said goodbye to my friend with a tone of resignation. Is that income that enables you to manage all your expenses the be-all and end-all of your life? Or is there something else you can do that you love? Something that will lead to a better quality of life and ultimately even more income than you'd ever dreamed up, precisely because you love what you do? The cash won't flow instantly, but it will flow eventually.

EXERCISE

Close your eyes and envision a perfect moment playing out before your mind's eye, like a movie. What are you wearing? What are the scents in the room or outdoor environment? How do others regard you?

_____

_____

_____

Determine whether there is any reasonable path from your current state, assuming nothing changes, that will bring you to this special "movie moment." Answer yes or no:

_____

Think about what that person in your mind's eye is doing or how he or she got there in the first place. Describe this:

_____

_____

_____

Determine whether there's a step you can take or a habit you can omit today that veers you closer to the activity of this future you. List it:

_____

_____

_____

Consistently check back in with this dream image as you make decisions. Ensure that the you in the movie would make the same choices you're making today.

This is how to become the future you over time.

CHAPTER 7

Exude Kindness

LEARN THE SECRET
ACCELERANT TO WEALTH

The first-generation Canadian real estate developer Sam Mizrahi started his career in the retail and commercial dry cleaning business by founding a company called DoveCorp. DoveCorp grew rapidly to close to a hundred stores before filing for restructuring in a bankruptcy court in 2007.

Early in the business's development, a customer brought a finely crafted and relatively valuable tablecloth that needed careful cleaning into the store where Mizrahi worked. Unfortunately, in the process of cleaning it, the shop destroyed the cloth to the point that it became unsalvageable. Not good.

Customarily, a dry cleaning store would simply issue the customer a credit for the value of the item and wash their hands of the ordeal. But Mizrahi took a different tack: without consulting with the customer, he scoured the market to find another tablecloth as close as he could to the design and quality of the original. Ultimately, he purchased a replica of the very same tablecloth for $1,200 and presented it to the customer free of charge. The customer was happy to receive the new tablecloth and grateful to Mizrahi for his consideration.

Twenty-two years later, Mizrahi was in the business of high-end real estate development, having founded Mizrahi Developments, which builds large, billion-dollar residential projects in Toronto. Talk about an iteration. Anyway, zoning and permitting issues are notoriously fraught with political and legal difficulties, and Mizrahi had to secure zoning approvals at a critical stage in a project's development. Serendipitously, and unbeknownst to Mizrahi, it turned out that one of the officials involved in the approval process was the very man who, two decades prior, had brought his valuable tablecloth to Mizrahi's shop for cleaning. In the midst of the hearing, the man turned to his colleagues: "This guy will do the right thing. He will do what he says." Mizrahi's zoning applications were approved, and a $1,200 gesture of kindness paid off in millions many years later.[1]

Kindness has a synergistic effect on society that allows the whole pie—the total sum of sharable wealth—to grow bigger for everyone. Kindness is a no-cost way to improve productivity, even during interactions with total strangers. Moreover, kindness is an expression of respect for someone else's time. Perhaps most importantly, a kind interaction that leaves both parties with positive emotions promotes a feeling of open-mindedness and creativity, according to, among others, the American Psychological Association.[2] A kind act might be receiving a free cup of coffee when you're in a rush or a multimillion-dollar windfall like Mizrahi's. Why would you pass up this opportunity to join the fun?

Consider Larry Stewart, a Kansas City entrepreneur known as the "Secret Santa." Between 1979 and 2006, during the holiday season Stewart doled out hundred-dollar bills to strangers who least expected it.[3] Stewart grew up poor and was down on his luck through most of his early adulthood. At a particularly low point in 1971, he entered the Dixie Diner in Houston, Mississippi, intending to "dine and dash." The diner's owner surmised that Stewart would be unable to pay and, approaching him from behind, pretended to pick up a twenty-dollar bill from the floor. He handed it to Stewart, commenting that Stewart must have dropped it—doing a profoundly good deed in a way that preserved Stewart's self-respect. Although impressed as he was by such an act of kindness, Stewart's luck didn't change much during the ensuing years: he was fired from two different jobs just before Christmas in 1978 and 1979.

Soon after his 1979 firing, Stewart noticed a young woman working very hard washing cars in ice-cold wintry conditions, and he thought to himself that surely she had it even rougher than he did. Out of the blue, and with his diner experience in mind, he handed her a twenty, to which, with tears in her eyes, she responded, "Sir, you have no idea how much this means to me." Perhaps that twenty bucks even saved her life, but we'll never know.

Then, the Secret Santa's fortunes started to turn. Finding joy in these random acts of kindness, he devised an annual holiday tradition to distribute money—usually one-hundred-dollar bills—to people in need. Meanwhile, he developed what became a very successful communications business and increased his gift-giving every year until his death in early 2007. One of his last charitable acts, reportedly, was to return to the Dixie Diner, where he gave the now-elderly owner and his ailing wife $10,000. Stewart once said, "I've been at rock bottom myself—thirty years ago I was an out-of-work salesman living in my car in Houston, Mississippi. I'll never forget the diner owner who gave me $20 for a good breakfast and a tank full of gas to drive out of town." Perhaps you're at an all-time low right now as you read this but see a path emerging in front of you. Do you think that maybe one day *you* will be handing out hundred-dollar bills like Stewart?

The very best business leaders today are those who are people-centric and transparent because they recognize that kindness is nothing less than the transactional "grease" underlying successful management and negotiation. Kindness promotes brand reputation and loyalty, employee productivity and retention, innovation and collaboration, customer acquisition and differentiation, and long-term stability.

We see corporate acts of kindness in various forms, including at Google and Microsoft, among others, where employee support programs offer counseling, mental health support, and resources for personal and professional development. Patagonia is renowned for its commitment to environmental causes. IBM encourages employees to work on community projects worldwide. Airbnb offers free housing to people affected by natural disasters or emergencies. The TOMS Shoes "One for One" model enables the company to donate a pair of children's shoes for every pair that's bought. AT&T sponsors employee education objectives. Companies like Zappos are known for their extraordinary efforts to ensure customer satisfaction. And Chobani gave away a 10 percent ownership stake in the company to its employees, making them potential millionaires if the company goes public or is sold.

But let's return to Larry Stewart, our Secret Santa. The companies I just mentioned are already massively successful, and one could argue that each deploys a version or two of a kindness program as branding exercises. Certainly, there's nothing wrong with that, but it's interesting to note that Secret Santa embarked on his anonymous gestures of kindness *before* he had much to give. Even more curiously, his commitment to charitable endeavors chronologically coincided with the growth of his unrelated business and a long-hoped-for rise out of poverty that enabled him, as we know, to be even more generous. In fact, his identity wasn't made public until well after many years of giving—the only reason Stewart identified himself, on his own terms, was because a media outlet was planning to publish his story.

We can draw a direct line of cause and effect in Mizrahi's story, that is, a long-ago kind act led to a specific financial windfall, but not so much in Stewart's case. Is it plausible to believe that Stewart's kind nature somehow led to his business successes?

I think the answer is yes. When you're charitable—whether it involves giving money or helping others in a variety of ways—and when you're not expecting anything in return, you experience a palpable broadening of your creative capacity. Some may call this your spirit or disposition. You're not holding on to your last twenty dollars as if it's the last bill that's ever going to enter your wallet. You're living a dramatic and transparent life on your own terms. And new ideas come to you when you're living in this way—a few of which may make you rich.

ACTIVE KINDNESS IS CREATIVE

Kindness is a form of creativity in its own right. And, to be clear, the kindness I'm talking about is not politeness. Being polite is relatively easy to do, but being kind takes intentional effort because it's giving something of yourself—your money, your time—to someone else. Being kind suggests an inherent, fundamental quality of consideration, compassion, and benevolence. It's a measure of character that is displayed consistently. To be "nice," meanwhile, is to be merely pleasant, agreeable, or polite in the moment—it's not a deep or inherent quality, and it's more about conforming to social norms and exhibiting courteous behavior rather than reflecting your inner disposition. Being nice is living life in neutral rather than in gear.

In the context of business, and in the parlance of the Really Rich, I think of kindness as strategic intent—*active kindness*. A deliberate act of giving provokes a shift in perspective to one in which you're not clinging desperately to either money or time. For some unexplained reason, it opens a channel for more fortune to pour in. For one thing, a person surrendering their last twenty dollars will make damn sure to be focused on iterating and reiterating to bring more money in.

Kindness is also not empathy. *Kindness* refers to the quality of being friendly, generous, considerate, and showing goodwill toward others. But an active kindness means to *act* in a compassionate and benevolent manner. You have to do something. Empathy, on the other hand, is the ability to understand and share the feelings of another. It involves putting yourself in someone else's shoes, being able to recognize and understand their emotions, and sharing in those feelings. Kindness is more about actions and behaviors, whereas empathy is about understanding and sharing emotions.

On an emotional level, an active kindness produces a low-risk environment, deactivating fight-or-flight mechanisms, which allows all parties in a negotiation, for example, to come to agreement a lot faster. It also promotes reciprocity in business relationships. The publicity strategist and author Jill Lublin, who outlines seven pathways to profit, goes so far as to claim that "kindness is the new currency" of the marketplace.[4]

If business is the act of making someone's life easier with a valuable good or service, doesn't kindness do the same thing?

KINDNESS PROMOTES BUSINESS GROWTH

James Freeman, the founder of Blue Bottle Coffee, started his coffee business in San Francisco because he was fed up with the taste of overroasted coffee beans from branded chain coffee stores—I won't name names. Understanding, though, that the coffee market was already saturated, with Blue Bottle he didn't seek to compete directly with the big chains but instead created a new and unique coffee-drinking culture grounded in "self-actualization," personal growth, and kindness. He correctly inferred that his market would be composed of people with advanced educations who live in high-income communities who would prize the perfection of the coffee-drinking experience. Among other branding exercises, kindness was at the forefront of Blue Bottle's largely word-of-mouth growth.

Videos, blogs, and social media posts emphasized the quality, sustainability, and quality control in the coffee's harvesting, storing, brewing, and serving experiences that made it a specialty product. The company's design aesthetic, symbolized by its literal "Blue Bottle," is minimalist, reflecting an exclusive, no-fuss, high-quality brand.

Most important, though, were the Blue Bottle point-of-sale innovations: it launched a no music, no Wi-Fi, and no computer policy at its cafés to encourage genuine face-to-face interactions between their customers and knowledgeable baristas.[5] Blue Bottle now has close to a thousand employees and a valuation heading toward a billion dollars.[6] It's safe to say, and it's certainly been my anecdotal experience, that the baristas working at Blue Bottle are happy ones.

Speaking of baristas, let's imagine a barista who is enjoying serving a parade of courteous customers. She's in a good mood, talking about all things coffee, doling out extra espresso shots, and smiling through her day until an onslaught of rude customers come in. As the afternoon wears on and she deals with increasingly rude people barking orders at her, how do you think her customer service is affected? It will naturally degrade, costing the coffee shop real dollars in upsells, repeat business, and online and word-of-mouth reviews.

Now apply this at scale, and you'll see two very different paths for society. Because humanity is economically interconnected, strangers benefit from each other's productivity and innovation, and so anything that thwarts progress is detrimental to the whole. Rudeness hampers growth. You can build an empire with kindness.

REASONS TO BE KIND

Who wants to be in an environment of rude people? For one thing, people don't enjoy a good quality of life when they hate what they're doing. Of course, the money may be good, so you stay in an unpleasant place because of various incentives. But you hate it.

If you feel your life is being misused, wasted, or misallocated, what you need, in a word, is creativity. I'd go so far as to say that if you're not allowed to be creative, it's like you're not allowed to be human. It's like wearing a dog collar on your brain. That's a punitive state of life. It doesn't matter that you have a comfortable bed or a nice suit on your body. An uncreative life is a prison sentence. Kindness is a powerful key to unlock these shackles.

Why be kind? Well, for one thing, throughout our careers, we're going to encounter various gatekeepers, people who have the sole power to determine whether you get what you want. On a basic level, you don't get into the nightclub if the bouncer doesn't like you, no matter how much cash you pull out of your jeans pocket. You don't get a meeting with a potential investor if the secretary thinks you're a jerk. You could be a bazillionaire, but if Beyoncé doesn't like you, you aren't going backstage to say hi.

Humans make the rules. So, if you want these things, if you want access, but someone else has the power to decide whether or not you get it because that's their indisputable domain, how do you have a better shot?

An active kindness allows you to get things done efficiently, plain and simple. This may seem obvious, but how many people have you worked with who are anything but kind? And how difficult are they?

Because there are so many insufferable jerks in the world, when you present yourself as someone enjoyable to be around, someone who respects others—whoever they are—for their time, contributions, ingenuity, uniqueness, and value, you'll be surprised how many doors open for you that you never expected. It's like a breath of fresh air. You're really not competing with anyone anymore.

Second, a lack of kindness forecloses your opportunity to make inroads, to build bridges with others who someday could help you. A guest on one of my podcasts called the infusion of kindness into his day as "preparing my battlefield." I think of it more as walking on a cloud. Sometimes you even unlock crazy cool rewards that you could have never imagined. Let me tell you, the busy restaurant always has an extra table ready for the Really Rich. Would you rather go through your day in a foul mood, provoking confrontation, or sail through your day having positive interactions—with everyone?

And by everyone, I mean everyone—the Uber driver, the parking attendant, the doorman, and those you work with and for. After I park my car in the morning, the next thing I do before heading to my office is buy an espresso. Recently, I've made it a habit to ask the parking attendant what he wants to drink as well—after all, I'm heading across the street to the coffee shop anyway and his coffee costs me just a few bucks. Meanwhile, this guy is effectively the only set of eyes protecting my multi-hundred-thousand-dollar car from abuse or theft. Through this lens, it's almost absurd *not* to offer the guy a coffee!

At first, the recipient of a kindness always has a look of incredulity: *Do you really mean that? You're offering me a cup of coffee?* Well, why not? What is it to me, maybe seven bucks out of my pocket? I especially enjoyed a recent interaction with a new very young valet, who initially couldn't believe my offer and wasn't even sure how to deal with it:

Me: Hey, thanks so much for taking care of the car. I'm heading over to get my espresso, what can I pick up for you?

Him: Oh, um. (*uncomfortable laugh*) No, I'm good.

Me: No, really, what would you like? It's my pleasure.

Him: (*looking around*) Uh, well, maybe just a black coffee.

Me: You sure? Just a black coffee?

Him: Yeah.

Me: Okay, see you in a bit. (*strolling across the street*)

Him: (*calling after me*) You know, if it's really okay, I'd love an iced mocha, with whipped cream and a chocolate drizzle on top.

Me: They'll make that in there?

Him: Yep.

Me: You got it.

It's so rare that new employees in relatively low-level service jobs find themselves treated like this that they don't even know how to navigate a simple offer. It was like I threw a turkey leg on the floor to the family dog who's been trained never to take scraps from the table; he wants it, but he hesitates. Is he allowed to have it? Is it really for him? Is this a deadly trick? It's up to you to show people that another paradigm exists where cool shit like this happens all the time. We all deserve a treat.

In the long term, who knows where these parking attendants will end up in relation to my life. In the short term, how much do you think I pay for parking, and who do you think has his car ready first? And in the moment, I start my business day with an open spirit, happy to have made someone's morning just a little better. You'd be foolish not to take this kind of thing for a test drive.

Then, in the coffee shop, I share a joke with the barista. We have a give-and-take: I make him laugh. He says something ridiculous. We both laugh. I pick up my two coffees and walk away. I feel like I was awarded something: I feel good. The barista is in a pleasant mood: he feels good too. The parking attendant gets something he didn't have to pay for. We've all created something valuable out of nothing but a few dollars and ten minutes of my time.

Now I'm primed and ready to get to work. I feel empowered to go hard on my mission for that day, whatever it may be. My touchpoints and initial interactions are all positive. I'm Rocky Balboa on home turf. I'm Ali entering the ring against Foreman. I literally feel fearless. In this way, I walk on a cloud. And you can too.

Was I fearless before I rolled out of bed? Not especially, though a morning workout certainly helped. The Dalai Lama offers an interesting insight in one of his teachings about compassion, suggesting that if you can't summon a compassionate Buddhist practice, then practice a self-centered one: by making yourself help other people, you'll actually feel much better yourself, even if the act of kindness isn't coming from a compassionate place.

An active kindness produces magical effects. I find that good things happen because I'm open to all the gatekeepers and opportunities for bridge building that come my way that day.

The ability to be kind and show a sincere interest in people is like gold. Or better, like diamonds: it's true value. It's you saying, "I recognize you. I recognize that you're valuable." And in turn, that other individual is going to respond in kind—the car will be waiting at the end of my day without a new ding on the door, the coffee is already prepared on a crowded morning. This, to me, is magical stuff. Imagine your own life with these added VIP perks around every corner.

Kindness promotes open-mindedness and creativity, and anything you can do to promote creativity assists you in iterating and ultimately succeeding. Moreover—and this is really beautiful—if you're being kind to others, which will always make them more open-minded in turn, you're helping someone else to solve their problems too. How insane is that? How valuable is that? "Thank you for being nice to me. I've realized that my day isn't actually that bad and that I can have fun working here and not everyone's an asshole and the world isn't as bad as I thought it was and I'm gonna be just fine."

KINDNESS CAN BE FREE

Kindness doesn't have to cost money—it can be as simple as extending yourself to help another. It just needs to be affordable for you to offer, whether it's hundred-dollar bills, a few-dollar coffee, or a well-placed compliment. A close friend of mine shared a story once about a former client, an accomplished sailor, who was painting on a quiet beach in the Bahamas. A young man approached him, seeming to admire his work in progress, and asked if he wouldn't mind sharing some of his brushes, canvases, and paints. A selfish painter might have thought, *I don't want this guy painting the same sunset that I'm capturing*, but the sailor wasn't that kind of a person—in fact, he was a kind person and happy to share some of his extra supplies. It didn't cost him a cent to hand over an extra brush that he wasn't using. The young man set himself up nearby and began his work.

After some time, as the sailor labored over his artwork, the young man strolled over to him to return the remaining supplies and gifted him the painting he had created—a portrait of the sailor in a neo-expressionist style. Impressed, the sailor thanked him for the gift and asked the young man his name. "Jean-Michel Basquiat," he said. Years later, needing to raise funds in a pinch, the sailor sold the work for several million dollars. How's that for a return on a simple kindness investment?

IT'S ALL ABOUT FRAMING

Rich Guy is looking for a fight, whereas Really Rich Guy is looking for consensus and win-win. Put another way, Rich Guy believes he can make his way through his world by taking what he wants and offering little in return. But in commerce, where the customer voluntarily hands over her funds for products and services, there's no such thing as taking without giving.

In a way, it's all about framing. A Really Rich gal walks into a salad bar that she goes to every day, and she makes small talk with the servers and tips them at the end of the transaction. As she continues to frequent the place, she finds she's not getting charged for extra items, or she gets double portions of what the servers know are her favorite ingredients. For everyone else, that extra helping of protein costs $2 more, but not for her!

A rich woman walks in to the salad bar next, offers the same tip, but says, "Pay attention, because I like my salad made exactly the same way. And if you get it right, you get a dollar or two extra." The servers will hate this second customer, even though the monetary transaction is precisely the same. So, is the value to be found in the money or in the relationship?

Furthermore, giving without expectation is the secret sauce, or dressing, if you will. In contrast, *if you do this, then you get that* is transactional.

The person who maintains a relationship over a long period always gets more out of it than a competitor who simply seeks to grease everyone with tips. You gain certain value from one-off transactions, but a relationship gets you access, gets the gatekeepers to open closed doors. Someone liking you pays off in multiples.

Given the nature of our economy, kindness more than ever is critical—people are keeping score. It's one thing to walk into Macy's and purchase a pack of underwear; that's a singular transaction, and you're unlikely to meet that salesperson or cashier again. But do it online, the way most transactions today are executed, and you're very likely to be peer-reviewed. This is a reflection of our tightening economic interconnectedness. A record is kept of every transaction, and a public score can be easily observed. Even an Uber driver is reviewing your performance as a passenger, as you review how he or she drives.

What was once invisible is now apparent. Back in the day, you could take a taxi after a few too many and vomit all over the backseat—oops, sorry. Do that today in any of the online car services and you may not get picked up again: every driver can now see you're a costly liability. And this rating system is only going to become more prominent as time goes by.

Your invisible attitudes are now being tabulated! That's what I would call a kindness quotient available for all to see. In the past, as a tourist you might have eaten at a restaurant where you experienced poor service and food and perhaps when you returned home you told a friend or two not to go there. Now you can broadcast that experience on Yelp or Google or any other social media site. And bad reviews over recent years have sunk a great number of businesses, large and small.

Amy's Baking Company, once featured on chef Gordon Ramsay's *Kitchen Nightmares*, became notorious for its aggressive responses to negative online reviews, which led to a public relations disaster and hastened the closure of its Scottsdale, Arizona, restaurant.[7]

In 2009, one single guitar player, Dave Carroll, depressed United Airlines' stock price after he posted on YouTube three protest songs titled "United Breaks Guitars," exposing his frustration with airline staff for mishandling his guitar.[8]

And a series of emails that went viral on X from one customer trying to order a PlayStation 3 controller ended up sinking a company known as Ocean Marketing. Notably, the company's representative was rude and unprofessional.[9]

Everything now is amplified, which of course cuts both ways. We can become Really Rich much sooner than we could have in the past, but we can also lose our shirts with even one stupid misstep.

Kindness—an active kindness—toward everyone is the guardrail preventing any such disaster. Are you underutilizing the raw power of kindness right now?

EXERCISE

Just because someone is doing their job doesn't mean they're not human. This week, implement an active kindness each day and see what happens. I can all but promise you that you'll be blown away by the possibilities this will unlock in an average week. Here are some ideas:

- Single out someone you pass weekly or daily and intentionally greet them with a hello.
- Offer a coffee to someone.
- Offer recognition for something you believe someone does very well.
- Lend a helping hand to someone who has asked for it—someone that you overlooked in the past.
- Thank people sincerely.
- Set aside a small amount of money to hand out each day to homeless people without questioning what it will be used for.
- Make a new commitment to recognize the people in your life you care about—with a letter, small gift, or gesture.
- Offer mentorship to someone earlier in their career or to someone with no professional experience.
- Remember people's birthdays.
- Compliment someone on something you feel they do very well—customer service, coffeemaking, or even their bright smile.

CHAPTER 8

Get Humble

HOW TO CROSS THE BOUNDARY
BETWEEN RICH AND REALLY RICH

THE COFOUNDER AND FORMER CEO OF SOUTHWEST AIRLINES Herb Kelleher was known for his outrageous personality. Once he settled a trademark infringement suit with a rival with an arm-wrestling match. Over the years, *Forbes* often referred to Kelleher as the best CEO in the United States, and Southwest to this day, unlike most other airlines, continues to enjoy remarkably high customer satisfaction ratings. Kelleher would say Southwest wasn't selling flight tickets as much as it was selling freedom—the freedom to fly. And for those invested in the company, there was also the freedom to get rich: a $10,000 investment in Southwest Airlines' IPO was worth $10.2 million thirty years later. Not a bad return on investment.

Kelleher, who passed away in 2019, left Southwest with an essential legacy—the notion that "everybody" is important. His "eight freedoms," which included the "freedom to learn and grow," the "freedom to create financial security," and the "freedom to create and innovate," helped to forge Southwest into one of the best places to both work and fly.[1] One company spokesperson called the airline's philosophy operating with a *servant's heart*: "We believe we need to connect people to what is important in their lives through friendly, reliable and low cost air travel. If you respect their concerns and needs, and still provide low-cost and low-fare terms, then you do indeed have a *servant's heart*. The customer, hopefully, is getting more than he or she paid for."[2]

Everyone is encouraged to be humble, but few are offered compelling reasons for doing so. The truth is that each of us understands only a small slice of our surrounding reality, and certainly no more than anyone else, which suggests that no individual has a sound reason to act lofty or arrogant. Tick off the names of top businesspersons widely regarded for their humility: Warren Buffett of Berkshire Hathaway, Satya Nadella of Microsoft, Doug McMillon of Walmart, and Indra Nooyi of PepsiCo, among others, understand that you need to practice humility to even be able to iterate and accept the responses or feedback that iteration provides. Otherwise, why would you bother going to the market to ask questions if you already know better?

A terrific example of how humility and arrogance can separate the fortunes of competitors is the narrative of the demise of Blockbuster. The undisputed champion of home video rentals in the 1980s, Blockbuster later collapsed for a number of reasons, almost all having to do with its arrogance from its perch as market leader. For one, the company abjectly failed to adapt to changing technology by turning a blind eye to the digital revolution and shifting consumer preferences. As streaming services and digital downloads gained popularity, the company's reliance on bricks-and-mortar rental stores and late fees became rapidly outdated. To make matters worse, Blockbuster was also burdened with a significant amount of debt, partly the result of its aggressive expansion and acquisition strategies. What once worked marvelously suddenly stopped working at all. For years after the threat from Netflix was apparent, Blockbuster failed to seriously adapt. As late as 2010, its CEO insisted: "I don't at all mean to poke any negatives at Netflix. I think they do a terrific job—at what they do. All we're saying is that we do something different, we do it really well, and that we have a really unique advantage....Call me brash, but we're building a world-class cross-channel distribution platform. Netflix can't deliver content the way we can."[3]

Four years later, the last of nine thousand Blockbuster stores closed its doors.

Netflix, however—the "humble" actor in this scenario—did everything the right way. Originally a competitor for market share with Blockbuster through its initial DVD-by-mail service, Netflix was aware enough to rapidly iterate based on perceived market changes, and it ultimately transitioned to streaming, which allowed users to watch movies and TV shows instantly online. The subscription model and lack of late fees appealed to consumers. Being able to order movies in your underwear without a trip to a fluorescent-lit, carpeted box in a bad part of town appealed to them too.

Further, Netflix invested heavily in original content and technology, diversifying significantly from its traditional rental model, which soon became archaic. If anything, Netflix today is the outcome of a series of bold iterations.

By the time Blockbuster tried to enter the online market, it was way too late—Netflix was already too dominant. In short, Netflix was humble, and Blockbuster was arrogant—it failed to iterate. The

CEO even gloated about it! From a Really Rich perspective, you can't even start to iterate unless you first understand that humility is a prerequisite for open-mindedness. After all, open-mindedness leads to successful iterations, and iterations lead to getting something big right.

ARROGANCE IS NOT CONFIDENCE

Arrogance inhibits new information from entering, thus reducing the speed of learning. In addition to narrowing your sphere of influence, arrogance, or assuming you know better all the time, is one of the most detrimental fatal flaws of enterprises and the leadership team that steers them. In a technological world of moving variables, little is held constant in the marketplace. Therefore, what's valuable shifts and changes: assuming you know everything creates a blind spot that can destroy the economic capacity of any business.

Arrogance is assuming that you and your opinions have a higher value and importance than what is true. Confidence is what you need instead, and there's a huge difference between the two.

Confident individuals have a positive and realistic view of their abilities. They recognize their strengths and achievements without belittling others. Arrogant people have an inflated sense of their own importance; they overestimate their abilities and downplay the contributions of others.

Confident people acknowledge their limitations and appreciate the skills and talents of others. They are generally supportive and encouraging. Meanwhile, arrogant individuals look down on others and dismiss their opinions while believing they themselves are superior. They struggle to acknowledge the value of others.

Confident people are open to constructive feedback and see it as an opportunity for growth. They can handle criticism without feeling threatened. But arrogant people reject feedback or become defensive in the face of critiques. They perceive criticism as a challenge to their presumed superiority.

Confident people understand that everyone has room for improvement and are willing to learn from others, whereas arrogant ones resist acknowledging their mistakes or learning from others because they feel they already know best.

Most importantly, confidence builds positive relationships, which are essential for a successful business. Confident individuals inspire trust and collaboration, which makes it easier for others to work with them. Arrogant people foster conflicts and resentment.

The arrogant may be rich, but the confident are Really Rich.

CONFIDENCE IS THE FOUNDATION OF HUMILITY

The most competent people are often the most humble; they are competent because they know how little they actually know about the field they're in. Ray Dalio of the hedge fund Bridgewater Associates famously opens his book *Principles* with this line: "Before I begin telling you what I think, I want to establish that I'm a 'dumb shit' who doesn't know much relative to what I need to know." The fact that someone as successful as Dalio knows this much is actually incredibly self-aware. The better we get at what we do, the more keen is our appreciation for how far we still have to go. Humility is the ability to understand how difficult it really is to perfect ourselves, to hone our products or services, and to achieve greatness. Meanwhile, the arrogant leader—think Blockbuster—surveys the scene and thinks, *My job is done here.* The Really Rich never, ever think that. Of course, the job is never done. Acknowledging how much more you have to learn is a good way to think because it's absolutely true.

In a sense, arrogant people view themselves like they're gods, which is ridiculous of course, because the difference between their intellect and their ability to process reality is nowhere near that ideal.

Some people have challenged me on this point, saying, "Well, what about Donald Trump? He's not humble." Setting politics aside, because that has little, if anything, to do with living a Really Rich life, my response is that I think he actually could have been a lot *more* successful in business if he was. He's actualized a fraction of what he would be capable of doing, and I don't put him on a Really Rich pedestal as some supreme example of success, despite the fact that he's benefited from a serendipitous environment of cultural abrasiveness.

Humility allows us to widen the scope of our open-mindedness. If our ability to absorb data is narrow, that means our spigot of information is tiny, and we can only process what we see, who we like, and what we already think. But when we're humble, we think, "I don't really know how to solve this problem, so let's bring in the scientists and the engineers and the consultants and the artists to inform me on how we can fix what needs to be addressed." Ultimately, multidisciplinary groups have solved the biggest problems in history.

Thomas Edison is considered to be perhaps the most prolific inventor the world has ever seen, but he had teams of assistants. One was Charles Batchelor, who played a huge role in developing both the light bulb and the phonograph. Another was the physicist and mathematician Francis Upton, who likewise helped Edison develop not only the light bulb but also electric generators and power distribution networks. Edison himself was self-educated; even though his mother was a schoolteacher, he attended a formal school only for a few months as a child. As brilliant an inventor as he turned out to be, and as much as he experimented throughout his life, Edison was humble: he knew he needed Batchelor, Upton, and many others to transform his visions into reality.

It's hard to find the truth of a matter, and it's harder still to calibrate the just-right iteration. Make it easier on yourself by listening for hints from others, from every perspective you can possibly get.

LEARN FROM LITERALLY EVERYONE

I recognize that not everyone is fundamentally humble—hell, I wasn't a humble person until I found myself at rock bottom in New Orleans. Getting your ass kicked really helps with this, and I highly recommend it. Better yet, don't start or continue your career thinking you know everything you need to know.

What happened to me when I went broke in New Orleans was that I realized my self-worth was tied up with a title and status that meant nothing anywhere but on Wall Street. I went from a Park Avenue apartment to a tiny bedroom in a shotgun house in a little town called Covington, Louisiana. The place was a hotbox of cigarette smoke and crumpled beer cans. I lived there with two guys who looked like they just got out of prison; one actually did. Here, explaining to people where I had come from just made things worse. It was considered a *negative* trait there to have come from such a haughty place.

Everyone is approximating their surroundings. Do you think your perception of reality is somehow completely accurate? Ten people viewing the *Mona Lisa* see ten different things. Everyone sees it slightly differently. So, in business, why wouldn't you want to gather as many viewpoints as possible to build your picture of reality, of how your world works? The parking attendant has something to say, as does the barista, the chef, the marketing specialist, the AI developer, and the CEO. The service workers understand, for one thing, how people tend to treat each other way more than you do. The AI developer has a better grasp of technology than you do, and the CEO presumably has more business experience than you do.

The richest guy in town may be the valet, not the banker. One of my most successful Rich vs. Really Rich videos depicted an employer refusing to hire a job applicant based on an interaction the applicant had with a janitor. People put on an act, they wear a mask when they're trying to secure something they want from someone they perceive as an important gatekeeper, but they act like their true selves around those who don't matter to them—such as a janitor, a valet, or a barista. After all, if you're a jerk to the valet, you'll probably be a jerk to me as well. It's just a matter of time. Do you really view us as entirely different?

I hosted a podcast recently with a big international banker who revealed that his bank would complete an interview process with their preferred candidate by inviting that person to play a round of golf. The individual naturally thinks he or she has secured the position. The bankers, meanwhile, don't care at all how well the individual plays—what they're looking for is whether the candidate swears and curses and kicks the cart or smashes their club if their game isn't going well. They want to see that person's true self in a stressful situation because if they act like that on a golf course, how could they be trusted with stressful multimillion-dollar deals?

We all have a filter that affects our tightly framed view of reality. Although some of our "windows" to the world are larger than others, each of us sees things subjectively through the filter of our experiences and how we've interpreted them. None of us is omnipotent. So, because we have a tight, little angle on the way the world works, wouldn't it be useful to see things, as well, through the frames of everyone else filtering past? Some of these views could be immensely useful, so why wouldn't you want to look and learn? If you don't listen to others, all you're saying is "I've already got the answer. I'm good. I don't want it." And your business growth stops right there.

Humility and confidence are in a direct inverse relationship with arrogance and insecurity: when you're humble, you're self-confident; when you're arrogant, you're masking insecurity. When you're a humble businessperson, you're a stronger one because you're more flexible. One of my favorite things to say in a business meeting is, "I have no fucking idea what to do," because that always results in a cascade of new ideas from everyone I'm working with. Moreover, people respect when a business leader can sincerely be this honest.

Admit when you don't know something. Of course, this might not be the best strategy for a general on the battlefield, but when you're engaged in developing a product or service, that's an intellectual war—and brains need time to create.

Who's succeeding in today's economy? It's the tech people, the former underdogs, the high school and college kids who didn't throw the winning touchdown pass, the kids who played *Grand Theft Auto* and *The Legend of Zelda* instead of going to the prom and getting laid. That's who's winning right now. The Y Combinator cofounder Paul Graham pointed this out twenty years ago in *Hackers & Painters*. I imagine these people have far less trouble finding a romantic partner these days.

Unlike previous generations, today's workplace expects and values open-mindedness and a willingness to test boundaries outside of the realm of how most of us were traditionally educated. Kindness is what underlies open-mindedness, and it's kind people to whom we're attracted in most business transactions. It's a small sample size, admittedly, but is it any wonder that the fewest deals made on the first ten years of *Shark Tank* were by Kevin O'Leary ("Mr. Wonderful")? And the most by Mark Cuban?[4] Who looks to be more fun to work with?

The key to success, as described earlier, lies in our ability to rapidly iterate. And to the extent that our time is limited, as we know, those who are humble enough to take in more information will maximize their iterative abilities and shorten the path before them.

Blockbuster failed because leadership lacked the ability to adapt. The newspaper business nearly collapsed because industry leadership likewise was almost mortally slow to adapt to the idea that people would prefer to read online. The major television networks—ABC, CBS, and NBC—were slow to react to the rise of cable TV. Indeed, one of the factors that caught the traditional networks somewhat off guard was cable's ability to offer a greater variety of programming and cater to niche audiences—which is exactly our viewing culture today. Cable TV allowed for the creation of specialized channels focused on specific interests, which attracted viewers who may not have been fully satisfied with the more general programming offered by the major networks. Eventually, the networks adapted to the changing landscape by diversifying their own programming, expanding into cable channels themselves, and developing strategies to compete in the cable market. But CBS was a full two years behind NBC's launch of CNBC and ABC's launch of ESPN. Having learned their lesson, and approaching the market in what would be considered a relatively more humble manner, each network now is aggressive in claiming streaming services market share.

In other words, humility can also be thought of as the self-awareness to know that the way you always did business isn't necessarily market-proof.

Passionate individuals with Instagram, X, and YouTube accounts often break news more rapidly than traditional news organizations. For one thing, such individuals on social media have developed trust with viewers, in part by understanding how social media works and in effect undermining the news industry's authority figures, who perhaps believe that "We're the boss, we control and sanctify the truth, and we've been doing this forever." In 2013, a BuzzFeed editor broke the story of the Boston Marathon bombing on Twitter by monitoring live police scanner transmissions. A passenger on US Airways Flight 1549 broke the story on Twitter that it had landed in the Hudson River—from inside the plane.

Individuals iterating on social media, if anything, *force* established media to respond. In 2016, the former football player Pat McAfee started a sports news and talk show on Sirius XM only to generate so much interest that some seven years later his platform is now distributed by ESPN in a deal reported to be worth "eight figures."[5]

In a way, this shows that traditional media isn't so much innovating anymore as outsourcing its innovations to the general public and then acquiring them under their umbrella to maintain their market positions. It's the little guy who opens new vistas for growth.

HUMILITY CAN BE NURTURED

Having a humble attitude, at first, may not come naturally to us. Certainly, it helps to suffer a huge fall as I did in New Orleans, but I don't particularly wish that on anyone—don't make the same mistakes that I did! But if you sense that you struggle to be humble, then it could take some practice. Let me tell you, once you're told to fetch a nine-and-a-half shoe for a customer when a year ago you were a millionaire bond trader, you'll find humility pretty fast. You can't bring your status with you everywhere you go, and so you may as well leave it behind entirely. Eventually, this way of living becomes second nature and your "resting disposition."

Arrogance simply doesn't produce the results you want. The drill is to not step on the next guy in your path because you're both trying to get to the same place. Rather, explore whether he knows something that you don't. If you disrespect him, he's only going to return that favor by disrespecting you. If you're devoting your efforts to preventing the other person from getting to where he's trying to go, you're negating your own path. See what you can learn from him instead—the result will either be helpful or neutral. But if you're rude to your competition, well, that's a negative. If you nurture a rude, arrogant environment, what ends up happening is you open up a third option: that the person actually hurts you.

In 1974 back at 3M, an employee named Arthur Fry came up with the idea of using a lightly adhesive, repositionable glue to create bookmarks for his hymn book. That idea eventually evolved into Post-it Notes. The idea for Amazon Prime, a program that offers expedited shipping to subscribers, reportedly came from a team of Amazon employees during a brainstorming session.

Humbly listen to everyone around you and see what happens.

EXERCISE

Great ideas come from cross-pollination with other vantage points. How can you better seek out the opinions of those you don't typically consider, and what would you ask them?

_____

_____

_____

Open your mind to the possibility that this person will offer an incredible solution to something you're struggling with.

Look for ways to apply something you've learned from this interaction.

Don't "hear" them based solely on politeness. _Listen_ to them.

CHAPTER 9

Don't Be a Jerk

WHY YOU MUST ABANDON RUDENESS

S TARBUCKS, ONE OF THE LARGEST SERVICE INDUSTRY EMPLOYERS in the United States and with thirty-two thousand stores worldwide employing thousands of workers, had a down year in 2020. This is primarily attributed, of course, to the onset of COVID and the lockdowns that affected most restaurants. But many stores remained open during the pandemic—and many Starbucks employees were loath to go to work because they found themselves serving lots of customers who were ruder and more abusive than in the past.

There were fights over complicated TikTok-inspired drink orders, shortages of product, evolving mask mandates, and problems ordering drinks through the Starbucks app—and people took it out on the baristas.[1] In some other stores, notably Walmart and Waffle House franchises, the stress became so heightened that police were called to manage violent threats.

The effects of being treated rudely during this period reverberated throughout the economy, with workers resigning in droves, causing service labor shortages. Polls of restaurant workers in 2021 showed that eight in ten quit their job because of customer disrespect. As it turns out, being treated like crap wasn't worth the money. Meanwhile, the US economy found itself more than two hundred thousand service workers short of the demand.[2]

The tales of rude bosses, once considered normal in the workplace, are legendary. Larry Ellison, the founder of Oracle, is described by his biographer as "a modern day Genghis Khan." And Jamie Dimon of JPMorgan is, according to the *New York Times*, a "famously bad listener," who routinely interrupts others.[3] Then there's Martha Stewart, who, despite her homemaking public image, allegedly had such a bad attitude that a Merrill Lynch brokerage assistant to whom she was particularly rude provided testimony that helped convict her of insider trading charges.[4] Perhaps Stewart would have walked if she'd had a rosier attitude off camera.

Such individuals may be fabulously well-off financially, but they're not Really Rich.

RUDENESS IS VALUE THIEVING

The range of behaviors from kindness through rudeness is symmetrical: if kindness is value-additive, and niceness or politeness is neutral, rudeness is value-thieving. Acts of rudeness can cost businesses huge sums of money. Poor behavior spurs an infinite chain reaction of losses in which even distant individuals lose. According to *Harvard Business Review*, among others, "incivility" causes nearly a 50 percent decrease in work effort.[5]

To make matters worse, rudeness, according to a recent National Institutes of Health study, is viral: suddenly, one rude value thief morphs into an army that can pull down even the most productive organizations.[6]

It's far easier to destroy than to create. Value thieving is a dark path that many are tempted to take when confronted with emotionally challenging situations. Accordingly, a fundamental understanding of this principle is more important for creating change than merely showing how ugly rudeness looks from the perspective of manners and common courtesy. Rudeness is selfish and a person's misjudgment of the severity of a situation. Rudeness can cost your business dearly and block the path to iteration.

Indeed, the most common reaction to, for example, seeing a customer screaming at an airline employee in an airport is laughter. That's because, from a distance, the person's misjudgment of the severity of the situation is much clearer to see than from within the argument. During an altercation, a rude person's behavior incorrectly asserts that their counterparty's feelings and needs aren't valuable. In that way, rudeness is dehumanizing. And that is never good for business.

Being rude to people you work with and to those you need to work with is like carrying a bag of bricks up the stairs. For an obvious example, think how even one bad online review about a restaurant or a small business can damage that establishment. The food might be great, but a rude waitstaff is considered inexcusable. Rudeness evaporates the one thing that everyone building a business wants: opportunity.

Just as there's a difference between active kindness and politeness, there are degrees of rude behavior. An active rudeness is antagonistic—there's a conscious disregard for others. But beware of passive rudeness as well—lack of eye contact, poor manners, out-of-context cursing, and the like.

WHAT IS RUDENESS REALLY?

Do you think you know what rudeness is? You'll be surprised by how subtle it can be. Here are some examples:

- *Verbal abuse:* Yelling, shouting, or using profanity when addressing employees creates a hostile atmosphere and undermines morale.
- *Insults and put-downs:* Belittling, mocking, or publicly humiliating employees erodes their self-esteem and diminishes their sense of self-worth.
- *Lack of respect for boundaries:* Some leaders may invade personal boundaries by intruding on personal time, making intrusive inquiries, or expecting employees to be available 24/7.
- *Unwarranted criticism:* Constantly nitpicking or criticizing employees, even when they're performing well, leads to stress and decreased job satisfaction.
- *Favoritism:* Showing preferential treatment to certain employees or promoting because of personal connections rather than merit breeds resentment and a perception of unfairness.
- *Withholding information:* Keeping employees in the dark about important decisions or developments within the company can lead to frustration and mistrust.
- *Ignoring input:* Dismissing employees' ideas or suggestions without consideration stifles creativity and motivation—this is the effect of not being humble.

- *Micromanagement:* Hovering over employees, scrutinizing every aspect of their work, and not allowing them to make decisions are demoralizing and counterproductive.
- *Discrimination and harassment:* Engaging in discriminatory practices or allowing a culture of harassment, such as racism, sexism, or bullying, creates a toxic work environment.
- *Lack of empathy:* Failing to acknowledge or support employees during personal crises or work-related difficulties leads to feelings of isolation and disconnection.
- *Unreasonable expectations:* Setting unrealistic goals or workloads without providing adequate resources or support leads to stress and burnout.
- *Retaliation:* Punishing employees for speaking up about workplace issues, whistleblowing, or trying to improve their working conditions creates a culture of fear.
- *Ignoring feedback:* Refusing to listen to employee concerns, feedback, or suggestions results in a disconnect between leadership and the workforce. This is fatal for all businesses, from the burger shack to the trading floor.
- *Egocentric leadership:* Focusing solely on personal ambitions and self-promotion, rather than the well-being of the organization and its employees, can lead to resentment.
- *Inconsistent behavior:* Leaders who exhibit unpredictable or erratic behavior can create confusion and instability within the organization.

If you're rude to someone, in a sense, you're essentially saying, "I don't see you as valuable. I'm abandoning social grace because I can't fathom how you could possibly be valuable to me." And if you've read this far, you know that is idiotic. Rude behavior fails to recognize that everyone is valuable and everyone has a unique insight and something unique to offer to the world. You're merely one vantage point; accessing more vantage points on the way the world works is like going from a stick figure to a Rembrandt. This is why I argue that rudeness forecloses opportunities to iterate most effectively.

Rude business leadership not only harms individual employees but can also negatively impact team dynamics, productivity, and the overall culture of an organization. Yet, amazingly, it's not uncommon.

Travis Kalanick was forced out of Uber, the company he cofounded, in large part because of his ruthless attitude toward competitors, employees, and Uber drivers. A video of him berating an Uber driver went viral, opening a very public window into his confrontational leadership style. And, of course, Elon Musk has a well-cultivated reputation for making extreme demands, such as once sending a scathing email to an employee who missed a company event to witness the birth of his child and, upon acquiring Twitter, issuing a midnight ultimatum to employees to commit to a work culture that will "be extremely hardcore. This will mean working long hours at high intensity."

Whether or not Musk is personally rude is debatable, but one can argue his Twitter ultimatum falls under the subcategories of "lack of respect for boundaries," "lack of empathy," "unreasonable expectations," and "egocentric leadership."

HOW YOU TREAT THE WAITER

At a party, I had a conversation with an investment banker who shared his bank's unique interview process. In the final round of interviews, after the candidate has been informed that they've "unofficially" got the job, the bank arranges to take the job seeker to a local diner. Not Le Bernardin, not Alinea, not Hayato—but a local greasy spoon in an area of Manhattan reserved for lost tourists. The kind of place you'd walk by and think, "Who the hell eats there?"

Of course, the senior guys know the waitstaff (and treat them quite well on these excursions), and they arrange in advance that whatever the job candidate orders they get the wrong thing: order the tuna melt, get a pizza burger, that kind of thing.

Then they sit back and watch how the soon-to-be employee treats the waiter. Is the candidate rude? "Hey, I ordered the burger. What is this crap?" Does the candidate not say anything at all and force down the plate of liver and onions? Or does the candidate instead say, "Excuse me, Donna, I know you're busy. I ordered the burger, but you brought me an omelet. Would you mind switching up my dish?" Which, of course, is the ideal way forward in such a situation—in the diner and in a deal.

The bank officials make the final decision right there.

And, believe it or not, some idiots fail this test! Some candidates are already out of sorts and having second thoughts because they're being taken to a diner rather than to a restaurant on the short list for the Michelin Guide. What the bank executives are looking for is insight into the candidate's behavior in an unusual situation. They understand that the way someone treats other people is a reflection of how that person is going to behave with clients when the bosses aren't around. The calculation is that the way the candidate treats Donna at the diner is the same way that individual will tend to be with coworkers and clients. This investment bank clearly places a very high premium on a lack of rudeness. This test is as close to perfect as I can estimate.

Another test I've heard about is a hiring company bringing a candidate out for an interview in another city. On the plane or train, the company has the candidate seated next to a plant, a passenger who will act difficult. How would you navigate that setting?

ADJUST YOUR VISION

We all know people who, for whatever traumatic reason, go through life believing that everyone's out to get them, that life isn't fair, and that it's a dog-eat-dog world: "I'm gonna be mean, because everyone else is." Our relationship with others is a mirror held up to ourselves. The truth is, when an individual is already tightly wound, lacks generosity, and probably has anger issues, he or she believes everyone else is, as well, and acts accordingly. Rich Guy in our Rich vs. Really Rich paradigm believes that everyone else is a "dick"—and this is why, primarily, rude business leaders aren't Really Rich.

The Stoic philosopher and Roman emperor Marcus Aurelius is famed for his self-restraint, sense of duty, and respect for others, so much so that the Roman historian Herodian praised Aurelius's "blameless character and temperate way of life." One of Aurelius's most famous quotes from his *Meditations* states: "You have power over your mind—not outside events. Realize this, and you will find strength." This is precisely how we can transform our rude tendencies into kind and humble ones. It literally is a choice we make.

There are most certainly days when I wake up and think it would be easier to cut corners, especially if I've been treated unfairly or cheated in some way. Just because we encounter scoundrels, morons, and chatterboxes, which is inevitable, doesn't mean we ought to become one as well. Thieves don't win in the end—they're unhappy, often broken, and certainly never Really Rich.

Like Marcus Aurelius, the Really Rich have standards.

Rudeness, on the other hand, is the refuge of the rich, because the rich, in the context of *Really Rich*, are actually insecure. Insecurity breeds arrogance. Arrogance limits a person's ability to be humble, to listen to others, and to iterate. Rudeness is essentially saying, "I'm not open to what's going to happen here, I'm not open to this negotiation, I don't want you in my space." In a sense, it's a transactional posture that springs from the delusion that the other party has nothing to offer.

You can't create value that way. When was the last time you flew off the handle and blew up a deal or relationship? Perhaps you don't even know you destroyed it yet. Don't be the banker yelling about a pizza burger.

EXERCISE

Write down the last time you were rude to someone and what happened:

_____

_____

_____

Describe how you felt in the moment or afterward.

_____

_____

_____

Did you end up getting what you wanted?

_____

_____

_____

Were you rude because of something they did directly to you or for something outside of their control?

_____

_____

_____

How were your repeat interactions with this person or business?

_____

_____

_____

Are you able to get away with this behavior because you believe this person to be a lower status than you? Or is it possible that, owing to the nature of someone's job or environment, they've misjudged you and you've misjudged them?

_____

_____

_____

_____

_____

_____

Have you considered that this person is more than their job title?

_____

_____

_____

Now, compare this interaction to the last time you were kind in a stressful situation. What were the results?

_____

_____

_____

_____

_____

_____

CHAPTER 10

Ignore Status

DISCOVER THE SUBVERSIVE BLOCKADE TO GROWTH

WHEN I WAS GROWING UP, MANY PEOPLE AROUND MY AGE were glued to the popular television sitcom *Full House*, where Rebecca (played by Lori Loughlin) falls in love with and eventually marries heartthrob and rocker Uncle Jesse, played by the still working and relevant John Stamos. It was *the* family show of the 1990s, and Loughlin's Rebecca became one of TV's most popular characters. In addition to her considerable earnings as a star of a major show, Loughlin also enjoyed a privileged status in the entertainment world, in the national media, and in her Los Angeles–area community.

In May 2020, however, Loughlin and her husband admitted that they, along with some fifty other people, participated in a conspiracy to commit wire and mail fraud in an attempt to bribe the University of Southern California with a half million dollars to accept their two daughters as fake rowing-team recruits. Loughlin and her husband were later sentenced to several months in prison and community service and ordered to pay hundreds of thousands of dollars in restitution. "I made an awful decision," Loughlin said. "I went along with a plan to give my daughters an unfair advantage in the college admissions process, and in doing so, ignored my intuition and allowed myself to be swayed from my moral compass."[1]

I would imagine that Loughlin, at the time, figured that all she was doing was using a portion of her fortune to give her two daughters a leg up in social status—USC is a difficult school to get into, with a current acceptance rate of about 12 percent of all applicants. I'm sure she also believed that they were smart, good kids, and she could afford it, so why not give them a little boost?

Indeed, other than money, social status is the alternative means by which a market applauds what it perceives to be valuable. And social status is also among the most powerful forces motivating individuals and businesses. If there is a spectrum with money and profit at one end and status and notoriety at the other, anything that's perceived of value in the market will receive some combination of the two (or sometimes exclusively one over the other).

STATUS, LIKE MONEY, IS NEUTRAL

Status, of course, isn't inherently a bad thing. Whether it's good or bad depends on how it's deployed. For example, social status generally provides someone opportunities to earn money because it provides greater reach, opportunities, and notoriety, but it also enhances that person's ability to influence people and world events. Nelson Mandela's twenty-seven years in prison, an unfathomable personal risk obviously undertaken with no expectations of earning money, generated enormous interest and garnered him worldwide acclaim that later provided him the authority to dismantle apartheid in South Africa and advance human rights in that nation. Similarly, the young Pakistani activist Malala Yousafzai leveraged her renown as a teen victim of a terrorist attack meant to intimidate girls from going to school to advance the cause of education for women in her country.

Whether an obsession with status is harmful or not, though, really depends on how a person views this social force. A desire for status can motivate us to work hard, which can lead to innovation, or it can foster unhealthy competition, undermining collaboration and cooperation. People often strive for higher social status because it can lead to advantages in various aspects of life, which include the following:

- *Self-esteem and identity:* Achieving a certain status, such as a prestigious job title or academic degree, can boost a person's self-worth and sense of accomplishment.
- *Motivation and aspiration:* Status serves as a motivating factor, driving people to set and achieve goals.
- *Happiness and fulfillment:* Although status can be a source of happiness and fulfillment for some, it of course doesn't guarantee happiness.
- *Improved mental health:* Achieving status goals boosts self-esteem and happiness, but the pressure to attain or maintain a certain status can also lead to stress, anxiety, and other mental health challenges.

Status is also purely contextual. In other words, it may mean something in one corner of the world and prove utterly useless elsewhere. I thought I was a big deal pulling down millions as a Wall Street trader, eating in the best restaurants, and wearing the finest suits, but that meant absolutely nothing when I was trying to nail down a blues gig in a New Orleans blues bar. In fact, it worked *against* me to the point that I hid it. No one wants to watch a fixed income trader play guitar—that meant you were a hack! Muddy Waters didn't start his career as a stockbroker. Money works just about everywhere. But high status in one place has no effect somewhere else. This is critically important to keep in mind.

In virtually every community, social status plays a significant role in how we're perceived and treated. It can impact our access to resources, opportunities, and social connections. Moreover, in some places social status may be highly emphasized; in others, humility and community values may be prioritized over personal renown. Status can provide material (e.g., wealth, possessions) or nonmaterial (e.g., reputation, respect) perks. And, depending again on context, people may place varying degrees of importance on different aspects of status. Whether Lori Loughlin's daughters matriculated at USC may mean something to certain Southern California business, social, and entertainment communities (it certainly meant something to Loughlin and her husband's self-image) but very little to the young women's future peers if they were to end up, say, working as surfing instructors in Bali.

THE ILLUSION OF LOWER STATUS

The Really Rich see opportunity in areas where others aren't willing to look. This includes, of course, being open to consider the opinions and ideas of those from a variety of social strata—not only those of their social class. After all, the feeling of superiority that comes with an elite status is, again, contextual and thus entirely imagined. For example, when you're looking down on someone you perceive as a lower status, what you're really doing is trying to confirm to yourself that you're not of that status. And that gives a rich guy, or someone striving to be rich, a license to be rude to those "beneath" them and a sycophant to those "above." Hence, why you may observe someone yelling at the airport clerk but changing their tune when they spot their bigwig client walking through the jet bridge right toward them.

It's all about attitude and frame of mind. You can justify staying in a swanky hotel because that's where you've future cast yourself to be, but to stay in a place that's way beyond your means because you think that'll impress people is the wrong motivation. Unless you're a Kardashian, have you reserved a private jet because that's the most effective use of your time, or are you flying on an ultra-luxury Flexjet because you're dying to post a picture of yourself in it on your IG feed?

To be clear, the Really Rich methodology doesn't offer a solution for wealth distribution or attempt to reengineer the mechanics of capitalism but instead points to perceived status as a culprit in modern society's woes.

At the same time, to be super clear, I'm not at all rejecting status. There's a reason it's one of the two rewards, along with money, that the market offers its successful players—it's a real measure of value. And, in context, a projection of status is a behavior that can be used to your advantage. Your awareness of what it is and how to wield it, however, is critical: on the one hand, status is valuable, but on the other, it's to your detriment to obsess over it or use it to judge other people and their entire worth based on this measure. The latter is a close-minded view, and you're unlikely to get the results you want harboring dismissive attitudes toward anyone.

When you're part of the "in-group," those of higher status, you have access, which opens more doors for you specifically in that group. But again, it's contextual. If you're the hotshot investment banker, you may be seated in the first couple rows at the Knicks game or you get to send someone to Nobu to pick up your lunch for you; if you are a badass blues guitar player, you're served your beer first at a New Orleans club. These perks are the spoils of excellence. What's interesting is that there aren't any perks to your in-group status in a different and unrelated group. You might have a PhD and tenure at a prestigious university, and everyone there fears you, but at the local bar, no one really cares about your titles. In fact, the guy at the bar buying drinks for everyone actually has a higher status there than the professor does. Imagine how ridiculous it is to see a rich guy fumbling with self-checkout at a supermarket shouting, "I didn't go to Princeton for this tedious crap!"

Once you're out in the street, whether you're the virtuoso guitarist, the hotshot investment banker, or the decorated professor, your status, for the most part, becomes irrelevant. You can't lug it with you as much as you'd like to. So carrying your status domains wherever you go and treating unrelated people according to the rules of your status circles is beyond stupid. Feel free to be a hotshot at the office, but when you're in another environment, you're in the woods with everyone else.

You can't read anyone else's status. So go ahead and be rude to whomever you want.

Until you find out you just insulted the CEO's wife in the elevator at an offsite.

STATUS IS A SOCIAL COMPACT

Perhaps your grandfather was a very successful man, and you're born two generations later with a certain renown attached to your name—even if you're a couch potato who creates little value. In medieval times, status was even more valuable than it is today. Status and title determined whether you could own property. Of course you may have had to earn that status by going on a Crusade or killing someone, for which a king would deem you a nobleman and award you with a portion of land, or you could have inherited it.

Even today, one cunning trick that people concerned with status play with each other is to distinguish between "old money" and "new money." Even when dollar amounts are the same, particularly pernicious individuals further qualify themselves as higher status by claiming they are "old money," meaning, in their view, their status is more valuable than that of more recent recipients of wealth.

HOW STATUS WORKS

Consider three models I've created that reduce one's temptation to rely on status: the Model of Interconnectedness, the Model of Equal Potential, and the Model of the Idea Economy. Each model makes a sound argument against relying on status for a sense of well-being and fulfillment.

First, the Model of Interconnectedness shows how bound humans are to each other, both for survival and for a sense of self-worth through comparison. Via the "Last Man on Earth" thought experiment—where you suddenly find yourself to be the last human remaining on the planet—your sports car becomes useless, as do flashy clothes, without a neighbor to impress. Would you opt for a Lambo or military Jeep in this strange predicament?

Buddhism, among other philosophies, has an elegant expression for such interconnectedness that goes back some three thousand years. The concept of dependent origination holds that bamboo reeds harvested from the field and bound into batches of sticks lean on one another so that each bundle stands, which makes it easier for a farmer to gather them without having to bend to pick them up. One batch can't stand without the others.

Second, a Model of Equal Potential demonstrates that, in an ideal free society, everyone should be evaluated for what they can accomplish, not for what they've *already* accomplished on an arbitrary timeline. Consider how teenagers in the 1970s were labeled as hippie potheads and how as they aged into adulthood they birthed the internet and created more wealth than previous generations combined. By not acknowledging everyone's equal potential, we also essentially turn off the spigot to iteration—your future is not written in stone.

Third, a Model of the Idea Economy is a thought experiment around how value will move from "doing" to "thinking" in the future, which will displace a significant number of experts and specialists who currently enjoy outsized social status. This means that less value will be placed on learned skills or specialization as we move forward in time, much like how the value of memorization has all but been eliminated with the advent of the search engine or Rand McNally map-reading skills with the advent of apps like Google Maps.

Everyone has the opportunity to raise their status and increase monetary gain if they apply themselves and iterate. You have the same potential as anyone else. And today, unless, I suppose, you're the 11th Earl of Sandwich, everyone's status is dynamic, all of us are in flux.

America itself was founded, at least theoretically, on the idea that each of us is free, each of us has a right to life, liberty, and the pursuit of happiness. We can argue, of course, the nuances of all this and how it has played out over the past 250 years, but this concept remains our founding vision. Perhaps ironically, the Founding Fathers sought to throw away all of this status nonsense when they pushed the British back to England, and then they attempted to enshrine it in our nation's founding documents. And they went through a heck of hard work and risk to pull it off.

At the very least, most Americans today resent unearned, inherited entitlement, whether it's the Kennedys', Bushes', Bidens', or Trumps'. And that's because, as a group, we'd inherently prefer to approach everyone as an equal. Think of the golfer who gives himself a little bit more of a beneficial handicap than his game deserves—he might find himself uncomfortably backed up against a locker in the mahogany-lined men's locker room before too long by an angry club member. One of the most hallowed American clichés is about being born on third base and thinking you've hit a triple—as much as we all strive for status, we also resent it.

If you're starting a business, you don't want to be resented. Who's the most hated person at work? The boss's son or daughter, that's who, because they aren't playing by the same rules as everyone else.

Ferrari has banned certain celebrities, reportedly including Justin Bieber, from buying their cars. First, he apparently lost his car for three weeks after a wild night out. Like you, I hate when that happens. Then he retrofitted the body kit and painted the originally white car an electric blue. He further adjusted or replaced other parts of the vehicle and then auctioned off the modified car without Ferrari's permission, which apparently broke some of Ferrari's first-year ownership rules. Game over, or whatever they say in Italian for when you're totally screwed. The Kardashians are also reportedly banned from future Ferrari purchases. I can't say that this doesn't provide me with a bit of grim satisfaction.

I would guess that either Bieber or the Kardashians have enough dough to buy out Ferrari and do whatever they want with the cars, but this is an interesting window into status exclusivity at the highest level. And it calls into question how real status is in the first place.

Wielding status like this moves you back to a zero-sum game. It's a way of gaining an unfair advantage over somebody else.

Consider again the Lori Loughlin scenario. She and her husband probably thought they were securing a place for their daughters at USC. But in effect their efforts were actually keeping two other deserving but unknown applicants from admission to the school, or in other words, from accessing the social status a USC degree is perceived to provide. And that's why so many people were so pissed off by Loughlin's actions. Of course, were this allowed to slide without a legal smackdown, it would degrade the entire institution of elite education in America. And we can't let that happen now, can we?

An expression coined in the 1980s describes those who pursue status to their ultimate regret: the Diderot effect. Denis Diderot was an eighteenth-century French philosopher who wrote a famous essay, titled "Regrets on Parting with My Old Dressing Gown," about the woes that befell him upon acquiring a new, fancy robe. The robe prompted him to upgrade his entire wardrobe, as well as his furnishings, made him feel superior to others below his newfound status, and eventually not only busted his budget but also brought himself profound regret. It's a slippery slope.

In this light, the pursuit of status itself is a zero-sum game, because there can be only one "king" of the mountain at any one time. Your gain in this game is my loss. And the pursuit of status never ends because you always want more influence than the next guy. The late entrepreneur and motivational speaker Jim Rohn perfectly summed up the Really Rich perspective on status in this regard: "The greatest reward in becoming a millionaire is not the amount of money that you earn. It is the kind of person that you have to become to become a millionaire."

Today, status—particularly educational status—has become less and less valued. In certain industries, you are not even required to attend college anymore. All Google wants to know is whether you can expertly code, and the technology company doesn't care so much whether you attended Harvard or Yale. A company like Google is essentially saying that employees' educational status no longer correlates with its revenue growth, so it's not going to worry about it. You can be a great coder with a community college education, and it's happy to snap you up. In this respect, making hiring decisions based on status is a false value.

In the tech world, the old status has become irrelevant.

In the real world, the key is to approach status as the Really Rich approach everything else—with humility, openness, and self-awareness.

> **Rich:** Where did you go to school?
> **Really Rich:** What can you do?

EXERCISES

INTERCONNECTEDNESS EXERCISE

Recall a time when someone of a higher status helped you:

_____

_____

_____

Recall a time when someone of a lower status helped you:

_____

_____

_____

How did each of these people benefit from assisting you?

_____

_____

_____

EQUAL POTENTIAL EXERCISE

Recall how you felt at your first job or gig:

_____

_____

_____

List five key areas of expertise that you now possess that you didn't then:

_____

_____

_____

_____

_____

Where would you honestly be today if you were judged on the performance of your first job for the rest of your career?

_____

_____

_____

Apply this to everyone you may interface with who is at an earlier stage or new stage of their career.

IDEA ECONOMY EXERCISE

Think about your "big idea" and how much you'd like to share it with the world or your customers. List all the ways you'd be able to build and share your idea using computing, software, and AI:

_____

_____

_____

Estimate how long it would take to get your first customer:

_____

_____

_____

Now remove technology.

Estimate how long it would take to get your first customer:

_____

_____

_____

Compare the two:

_____

_____

_____

CHAPTER 11

Lean on Creativity

HOW TO BECOME
FUTURE-PROOF

FROM A REALLY RICH PERSPECTIVE, *FUTURECASTING* IS another word for the creative vision each of us, as individuals, must have to manifest the sort of life we want to live. It is the destination we're individually striving for and the goal of all the hard work and iteration. Without a future-cast model, and without knowing what our target is right from the time we set out, there's no way to sustain the iterative process. I'm not suggesting that your future-cast model can't ever change—of course, it can, because this is a result of the creative process and the effect of iteration—but we need to have that "brass ring" to reach for at all times. You're lost in outer space without it.

EVERYONE CAN FUTURE CAST

You don't need to master computer science, social science, statistics, or psychology to engage in futurecasting—you only need to know (or have a rough idea of) who you are. Futurecasting is the act of creating a vivid description of where you'd like to head without having the faintest idea of how you'll get there. The how isn't important right now.

With at least a preliminary notion of who you are, you're ready to create your ideal destination. The idea here is to pick a single moment and build it in your mind's eye (or on paper) as richly as possible.

- What is your dream moment?
- How do you feel in this moment?
- How do others regard you?
- How do you look and carry yourself?

It's helpful to return to this vision over time so it increases in resolution and emotional intensity. And don't be afraid to mold and refine this vision as you try new things and previous desires are experienced as disappointing.

When you shape where you want to go, with all the signs and sounds that accompany your desired destination, the unrefined present might look even more ugly and frightening. Life is terrifying enough—we don't need to go about making it darker and more foreboding for ourselves.

Let's pretend that our future cast involves earning a vast sum of money. Should we resign ourselves to being unhappy until we attain it? In order to not sign a contract with misery, we must take inventory of the things we can enjoy right now, the things we can treat ourselves to in the present moment. Even a simple walk away from your desk for a coffee is really a luxury, to the new hire and billionaire corporate raider alike.

Your present inventory to enjoy may look like this:

- Walking in the outdoors
- Making homemade cookies
- Talking with a friend

Future inventory to enjoy:

- Traveling to a luxurious beach destination
- Wearing a fine suit or couture dress to the Met Gala
- Buying a family member a new, more comfortable home

And here's the key that most people miss: with an inventory of what to enjoy now, we must ensure that we actually enjoy it! Don't skip the long phone calls with a friend or perfecting your chocolate chip cookie. These available rewards provide precious fuel for us to continue on our Really Rich journey with an optimistic outlook.

YOUR FUTURE WITH ARTIFICIAL INTELLIGENCE

Our culture and economy are already deep into an artificial intelligence revolution—2025 evokes 1993, the year prior to the widespread use of email and the introduction of online payment software. Memorization, specialized skills, and certifications will become all but useless in a near future supported by advanced AI and robotics. We've seen how quickly the world of traditional education has been transformed by the internet and its global repository of information, not to mention the advent of virtual classrooms. These trends will be accelerated by a humanlike AI and its ability to rapidly sort through and reorganize information.

This vastly democratizes *who* can get rich by empowering idea creators rather than incumbents or holders of expensive degrees. Essentially, many incumbent leaders in society are nothing more than "skill squatters," who through their ability to fund a costly education have been given access to certificate-based employment opportunities. Even high-skill areas of medicine, such as MRI diagnosis, are ripe for disruption with developing AI. If you're sitting here thinking all the opportunity is gobbled up, you couldn't be more wrong.

This is problematic for the privileged incumbents but empowering for the next generation of thinkers who will be unburdened by the costly ritual of grad school, formalized testing, and sitting in a dusty lecture hall. This is a very good thing.

By embracing the power of AI and placing less emphasis on memorization or specialization, clear thinkers from all walks of life will build valuable technologies, art, and communities—without capital or deep experience. And when the value of memorization or specialization decreases, the values of innovation, originality, and sheer creativity skyrocket.

Think about it. The transmission of information and ideas accelerates innovation. Innovation further accelerates the transmission of ideas. So this idea of singularity—the scary, imagined point when technological growth becomes uncontrollable and irreversible—is realized when we've developed an AI that innovates upon itself in a frictionless and virtually costless way. Certainly, humanity—the toolmakers—still has to think and chat and make video calls, and maybe we have little links between our brains that are still relatively slow, but robots can iterate instantaneously at scale. Imagine having the power of an entire population, an entire city, working on your math homework and sharing the answer instantly. And imagine what the singularity is when machines talk to each other at such a high caliber and at such an incredible speed that we "crash up" in terms of innovation, and, just like that, everything from hunger to water shortages to environmental destruction to cancer has been solved.

Such "science fiction" raises the boogeyman of autocratic control, perhaps not unreasonably. After all, many intelligent and prominent voices already warn about the advent of an uncontrollable AI, including Elon Musk, a cofounder of OpenAI, who at one time referred to AI development as humanity's "biggest existential threat"—which is saying a lot. Before his death, Stephen Hawking suggested that AI could "spell the end of the human race" if not properly controlled. Similar warnings have been issued, as well, by Bill Gates and the authors Stuart Russell and Max Tegmark, about what can happen if AI fails to be responsibly developed.

But here's what's really at play if we're talking about democracy versus an authoritarian future. Democracy and capitalism tend to promote open-mindedness because thinkers and doers require the liberty to study and act. Those in autocratic societies generally don't enjoy such privileges. Moreover, capitalism, with its hands-off approach relative to a state-controlled economy, rewards innovation in a super-incredible way via profit and notoriety. No one in North America, at least for the foreseeable future, should realistically expect a knock on the door that takes their company away. Of course, if that were to happen, innovation would grind to a halt.

THE REWARDS OF FUTURECASTING

The rewards for getting these groundbreaking technologies right are enormous because the innovations are so valuable. The individuals building OpenAI, for example, didn't just release one model and say, "All right, guys, that's it." OpenAI now has multiple models, and a new one comes out almost every other month. In other words, they're iterating to create the perfect model for different types of solutions. One model does math, one model writes code, one model writes poems, one model chews through images, et cetera. And to get this right, hundreds of thousands of pieces of software are being built on top of it. OpenAI's engineers and scientists are motivated by the value the product creates.

Artificial intelligence scares many people, but so has everything that's new, unknown, and inexorably coming. AI does present several potential challenges, but it also unveils an overwhelming promise for potential benefits that each of us can exploit. Most of all, AI drastically shrinks the time traditionally needed to envision, create, iterate, and market a product. And shortened time is the best news possible for the Really Rich.

Job displacement is going to be the biggest social interruption as AI further develops and becomes commonplace. But, let's face it, this is the effect of every major technological advance: the printing press lessened the need for scribes but created the publishing industry, not to mention the dissemination of a vast amount of human knowledge; the steam engine not only precipitated a social transformation from agriculture to industry but also replaced the need for blacksmiths, grooms, farriers, and stable boys with opportunities in specialized mechanical skills; electricity created millions of new jobs while diminishing the whaling, candle making, ice harvesting, and hand-washed laundry industries, among others; the development of the automobile put the final nail in the coffin of our horse-dependent economy; and the advent of the internet killed travel agencies, photo development shops, the typewriter business, and the encyclopedia industry, to name just a few.

All these epochal innovations created far more value than what was lost—that's why the market responded positively to them and why such relatively modern cutting-edge fields remain so successful. Can we even calculate how much value was created by the automobile or commercial flight? The computer and the internet are themselves the fount of so much of the wealth that's been generated over the past forty years. AI will likewise decimate certain industries we will no longer need to rely on—that's just the nature of technological innovation.

If you're worried about privacy concerns and security risks, well, let's be honest: they're already watching us, and, yes, it's only going to get worse without proper regulation. But this alone is not going to stop AI innovation.

So, what does AI do? It basically takes the power of the computer that we've enjoyed for years and multiplies that by a thousand—or more. Ultimately, all the things these machines we're building will do is extend the limits of existing human capabilities. Hey, I can move around on my own, but now I can get there faster! Hey, I could do the math on my own, but now I can do it a hundred times faster by performing a thousand math problems at the same time! All of this flows from the historic human yearning for efficiency, control, and expanded capacity.

AI enables us to make more complex assessments and to move even faster in the direction that we choose. You don't have a photographer available? Just create an image by typing in a few lines. Don't have a translator? Google (today) can create your Spanish transcript. You're running out of excuses for not getting your business idea off the ground. These are small tasks that once customarily required help from multiple people. For every bus driver job likely to be lost at the advent of driverless public transportation, hundreds of new jobs will need to be filled to maintain and iterate on the new technology.

In the end, the printing press empowered the individual to study, read, and write. Electricity powered not only industry but also advances in health and leisure. Setting aside the real costs of fossil fuel impacts, the combustion engine, the car, and air travel gave rise to the suburbs and individuals' ability to move freely across the globe. And the personal computer empowered us all to communicate with ease, among many other benefits. In other words, despite some temporary pain to certain workers, the coming AI revolution promises to benefit the liberty and freedom of everyone in the world. I know that this is counter to current AI doomsaying, but to me, on the basis of historical precedent, such future growth is rather obvious.

If anything, the personal computer and the internet are returning sheer power to the individual. The question is, as with everything, what are you going to do with it? Have you used your car to rob a bank, or did you use it for economic good? AI poses the same challenges.

We can exploit AI to extend our own ingenuity further than we thought possible. And, really, the only social constraints we face come down to human morality and creativity. When we're contemplating how to employ AI or any other tool, there must be a good intention to get something useful done behind it—after all, a hammer is a neutral object: it can be used to put a nail in the wall or to knock someone over the head. Like everything else, a simple hammer presents a moral dilemma: to be used for good or for evil.

Yes, the unknowns of AI are perhaps more widely distributed than those of a hammer or even an automobile. The "hive intelligence" that AI promises theoretically could lead to artificial "brains" that make decisions on their own. We've heard such scare tactics before: the calculator will make our students stupid; Google Maps will cause people to lose their natural sense of direction. But who still enjoys doing arithmetic by hand or remembering how to get to their favorite dim sum spot in Queens?

In the eighteenth century, when the sun set you went to sleep. If you were wealthy enough to have candles, or had access to a flensed whale for fuel, perhaps you stayed up later than most. If you were really loaded, maybe you could stay up and drink until you passed out. In a city, you were asking to get your head knocked in just walking down a dark street at night; in the country, any sort of wild animal might jump out and attack you. Once we could easily see at night with electricity, however, the entire economy was transformed—we could both work and consume twice as long as before. Electricity stimulated production and led to vastly increased economic output. All this from a glowing metal filament in a little glass bulb.

Well, a critic might say we're not sleeping as well anymore. Yeah, but we're not sleeping on a bed of straw over packed dirt either. In fact, you can have an organic wool and cotton mattress arrive at your door tomorrow. Just cut open the pressurized plastic sealant and you're ready to count sheep.

All this innovation springs from futurecasting, and all of futurecasting springs from creativity. The story of electricity's development is nothing more than the story of continuing iteration, from Franklin to Watt to Faraday to Morse to Edison to Westinghouse to Tesla to Einstein to Musk. The human spirit infuses every innovation, including, of course, AI.

GET STARTED

You cannot afford not to future cast—the future is iterating right before your eyes. What value can you create to both exploit what's about to happen and contribute to this economy in a meaningful way?

Start from where you're at. What are you interested in? What can you uniquely provide or lend a hand at? Soon enough, and for some industries right now, you will be able to lean on AI to build a prototype of your business extremely quickly. Indeed, you can use AI to sell something that has nothing to do with AI. You can use AI to create crazy art that's framed and mailed to consumers, you can use it to do someone's taxes, you can use it to write, send, and respond to mass emails. AI is flexible and agnostic. You can tweak it and build on top of it. It's like retrofitting a Ford to be a race car or, instead, redesigning it to move chickens around. Getting comfortable with AI is the name of the game right now—comfortable using it and comfortable acknowledging its value.

AI allows you to leverage your own unique skills. If you're a scriptwriter, it can learn your narrative style and draft a countless number of other stories. You can do it again and again with every new idea.

Before, we were individual beings who relied exclusively on our own talents and ingenuity, but now we can engage with the totality of human thought. You can replicate yourself, which means you can be more you, you can achieve more of you, through AI. All of this frees up your time, which is always the goal of technological revolution. Liberate yourself from rote and routine repetitive actions so you can jump into different tasks.

I handwrote the first Rich vs. Really Rich videos, but now many of my scripts, which have a certain formula and tone reflecting how I view and interact with people, are augmented by an AI I repurposed for this task. This is called *multishot prompting*. You identify who you are and give the program an example of what you do or how you write. The AI will spit out a draft, and of course you might need to modify it, and then you plug that back into the program. In my case, I end up with a modified version—some original, some AI-generated—and I can then create infinite twists on whatever theme happens to intrigue me. Specifically, the AI used a script I had written about a character who slips and falls, and it came back to me with a new take on it. All this is currently available through the large language model (LLM) of your choice.

For me, and for many others, OpenAI is like a playground where I audition different models and ideas and essentially toy with them. The speed of my development, therefore, has exponentially increased. Do you think anyone can cry writer's block anymore? Of course, there are all sorts of settings and adjustments you can make in real time to control the dispersion and tone of information—because you have to direct the randomness—but the output is instant, and the creative process, at least in my experience, has been wickedly effective. Technically, I can right now create Rich vs. Really Rich skits forever, without ever filming one, and I can continue such production even beyond my lifetime.

Technically, we could resurrect your favorite sitcom from any era and do the same. I imagine some savvy developer will pull this off sometime soon.

Futurecasting is the last of our ten Really Rich behaviors not because it's the least important—indeed, none of these behaviors is least important. We create value, in part, by keenly understanding that time is precious; we optimize for quality of life rather than targeted dollar amounts or status obsessions; we iterate effectively by remaining humble and kind and tuning our products or services to what the market decides is valuable; and we future cast both to know where we're going and to achieve the dreams we set forth for ourselves.

Utilizing each of these behaviors is the only way to become Really Rich in our contemporary economy—there is no other surefire method. This is the crystalized formula of what it takes to become a successful entrepreneur today, to live freely, and to create the unique life you envision for yourself.

A Non-Fear-Mongering Guide to the Beneficial Use of Artificial Intelligence

- AI is simply probability—it makes good guesses. It's not an oracle.
- AI is based on generalized knowledge, not specialized knowledge, that humans themselves have already discovered and programmed.
- AI output should be considered as raw ingredients, never the finished product.
- The first idea comes from you, not an AI.

- AI can help you validate your idea, but it won't validate it for you. Real people in the market are always the ultimate validators for a new product or service.
- AI highlights opportunities you may have missed, but they still need to be tested.
- AI is no excuse to become lazy and detached from your mission.
- AI may eventually take everyone's job *except* those of the entrepreneurs and thinkers.
- Applying AI too early in your workflow will lead to increased confusion.
- You still need to know how and what you want to do before applying AI—it's not a magic bullet.
- Familiarize yourself with what AI can and cannot do to support your idea early in the process.
- Using AI without intending to create value doesn't create value.
- AI should save time; if it doesn't yet—don't use AI.
- If you were to abandon oversight of your business, AI wouldn't save it.
- AI is a reflection of your perfection. Do not seek to be a reflection of an AI.

CHAPTER 12

Demonstrating
the Principles

W HEN I WORKED ON WALL STREET, I HAD A HORRIBLE DIET,
primarily because of intense stress. Of course, I was working nonstop, and any time I may have had to prepare a decent meal
was time away from making money—I was rich then, not Really
Rich. Eventually, I'd find myself disgusted with my persistent anxiety and extra flab, so I'd decide to lose the weight and get more
exercise.

To drop pounds in a way that sticks, there are, of course, certain
recommendations you have to follow. You set yourself a goal, obtain
information about eating nutritionally sound meals, stick to your
meal plan, exercise, drink enough water, get enough sleep, have the
patience to lose weight gradually over time, and stay flexible enough
to change things up as necessary.

If you follow that formula, barring medical issues, the weight
will start to drop off, and you'll begin to feel better. But if you do
only a few of these behaviors, your weight loss will stall or possibly
not work at all. For example, you may eat well but never get up off
your couch—that probably won't work. Or you might spend five
hours at the gym and then polish off a couple of lasagna entrées

with tiramisu for dessert—that's not likely to work either. As always, each person's approach to their health and well-being is entirely up to them. We all have the power of choice when it comes to personal wellness.

Likewise, the most empowering aspect of the Really Rich system depends on choice. On a fundamental level, everyone has the ability to select which path to walk as they go about their day: bloodthirsty and fierce, or flexible and open-minded. Or, according to this methodology, Rich or Really Rich.

By now, it should be obvious that you don't need excess resources, like money, to embody the traits of the Really Rich. Although economic windfall is common to the Really Rich, there are advantages to the Really Rich mindset that can't be measured in financial terms.

You may have read through each of the behaviors and thought, "Well, I'm good at certain of these, but maybe I need to show more active kindness," or "Maybe I've got to be more conscious of time— so I'll focus on these one or two elements." But this isn't a tapas menu from which to pick and choose items to experiment with while on vacation in Madrid. I'm not offering you a selection meant to pique your interest in certain business or lifestyle strategies; I'm handing you a gold-plated opportunity designed to persuade you to buy into this approach whole hog. The Really Rich approach is an organic system of doing business in a way that will not only make you rich but also nurture precisely the sort of lifestyle you imagine for yourself.

If you're working at a salaried job that you resent and pine for the weekends, when you host notoriously fun charity piñata parties, ones where maybe you met your significant other, well, maybe there's something you ought to explore about expanding the aspects of your life from which you derive the most happiness.

Now, I'm not suggesting that you shouldn't immediately pick up the one or two behaviors that most intrigue you and take a few swings to see how they feel in your hands—it is a challenge to transform a complete ten-point system into practice. But maybe start with your own future cast—where do you want to be, where do you want this bulletproof system to take you? A Really Rich life is going to monumentally change things for you, forever. And learning how these behaviors work together and complement one another will hone you into a more equipped, intelligent, compassionate, and successful person. Because now you don't have only half the story about how to lead a fulfilled life—now you have the full story about what guarantees success.

I've posed a lot of questions in this work. The main point is for you to sit in a quiet room and come up with the answers that are right for you.

- Who do I want to be?
- What sort of lifestyle do I want to live?
- What does that look like?
- How do I get there by making a small step today?

The stakes are high—it's your life. When I suggest you need to strategically apply kindness, I'm not talking about fairy-tale kindness, the kind you read about in fables as a kid. I'm talking about billion-dollar kindness, life-changing, kickass kindness that's neither soft nor squishy. Understand what *iteration* means—it's a serious discipline. Do you really understand value? Are you keenly aware of the limits of time?

Nevertheless, part of what made the Rich vs. Really Rich video series so successful was that viewers easily grasped how simple and logical it is to switch sides—you can go from Rich to Really Rich with only modest behavioral adjustments. Rich Guy is an appealing heel, not because anyone really wants to live like him but because he's so perfectly, comically wrong. Meanwhile, Really Rich Guy is who we all aspire to be, the way we all want to act, with the realization that it's entirely possible to do so. And changing behavior doesn't even cost you a cent.

HOW THE BEHAVIORS WORK TOGETHER

Perhaps the service industries are so vulnerable to customer rudeness because of the natural power imbalances embedded into the dynamic—some customers feel they don't have to be kind or polite. The consequences of acting like a jerk in a Starbucks are far less than they are when you act like a jerk in a board meeting or in most work settings. After you're rude to the barista, you just grab your cup and walk out the door. But if you're rude to the guy across the desk, they'll kick you out of the meeting and tell you to go pack up your stuff into a cardboard box. What Really Rich is saying, at a profound level, is to be intentional about active kindness when nobody's looking, even when the power is imbalanced—even when you think (wrongly) that you can get away with it. Such genuine behavior, in this case, the changing of your default setting to kindness, is part of what makes you Really Rich.

This book is composed of the basic, costless ways of adjusting behavior so that you can consistently interface with the outside world to pull out as much value as you possibly can in a fun, harmonious way. These are the ways to get the most out of life without spending any money on gadgets or courses.

Applying these behaviors is also the fastest way to earn a ton of money as pleasantly and as effectively as possible. Plus, this method enables you to become rich while having fun at the same time. A cutthroat approach might work for you once, but it's not a consistent money-making strategy over the long run. The Really Rich way leads you to wealth by building on the foundation of finding and expressing your true self. This brings calm and confidence to your business development, not to mention the deep satisfaction of having carved your own path.

Moreover, you don't have to look over your shoulder. Rather than cheating and stealing, living the Really Rich life is the only way to sleep soundly at night.

To the reader who thinks, "Screw having fun. I just want to make money," I'd kindly suggest you do some serious futurecasting to reassess your priorities. Because what's the point of having a lot of money if you're going to be unhappy? You have to think this through. Do you want to be rich but miserable? Do you want to be rich but outcast, rich but hated by everyone around you? To paraphrase Mike Tyson, if you think having a lot of money alone will change your life, then you've never had a lot of money.

Look, this is exactly the perspective I had when I first started working, fresh out of college knowing nothing, but look at how that turned out—the years of twisting and turning I had to go through to get myself on the Really Rich path, to earn back my autonomy.

For those who want to seek wealth and f*** everything else, I have news for you: eventually, that's just not going to work.

And for those of you who realize this already, *Really Rich* is exactly the book for you. Come on down, join us! This book aims to show you not only how to get from Point A to Point B but also how to have the awareness that Point B isn't exactly what you thought it would be.

It's an utterly losing proposition to say I'm going to care about *that* when I get *there*. No, the correct route is to care about *that* now in order to get *there*. Not only is that the surefire method to get there, but also you'd better start embracing the things you care about now because, when you get there, you're going to find yourself somewhere other than where you expected to be and you may not be much closer to the things you thought you cared about. In fact, you'll almost certainly have dismissed the things you once cared about. Ask any rich person you know: this is 100 percent guaranteed.

And what do wealthy people do once they come into their money? First, as is human nature, there's a consumption phase—we get all the stuff we always wanted. But eventually, after that, we all reach a level of understanding that one can only have so much stuff. We start to think about new challenges at work for the sake of the challenge. Maybe we start a new hobby. Very wealthy people might want to build a school or even a hospital wing. These are the goals that become important—more important, even, than making money. At the end of the day, all wealthy people, whether they're rich or Really Rich, chase the same thing: they want to spend more time with their family, they want to spend more time with their kids. But here's a caution sign: if you devote yourself to the "f*** everything else" technique throughout your career, you'll be extremely fortunate if any of the people you suddenly now remember that you love want to spend any of their time with you.

Many older rich people share the same observation: the money is less valuable than the dreams that got broken along the way. Recall our lottery winner, Jack Whittaker. At the end of his life, he wished he'd never had all that money in the first place.

Please don't misunderstand me: I love making money.

Money is very important to me.

But this may be the most essential lesson in this book: money is less valuable than other things.

Therefore, by prioritizing the other things that are important to you—and each of us is different, with a wide variety of needs and desires—you won't lose these heartfelt dreams but they will become the very springboard to your wealth, happiness, and success.

I learned this the hard way, but you don't have to. Now that I'm successful and happy in what I do, I realize that money is less valuable than how I spend my time. I've learned that lesson, and my businesses are thriving as a result.

ALL THE BEHAVIORS ARE IMPORTANT

No one behavior in the Really Rich kit is more important than any other. I could say kindness is most important, but if you make kindness your exclusive behavior and you fail to, say, iterate, well, then, you might as well become a monk. If you iterate while being rude to others, you'll be spinning your wheels and getting nowhere. If you don't future cast, you can iterate all you want, but you'll do this for the rest of your life because you won't have a target. If you fail to appreciate the essential, limited nature of time, you'll give in to laziness and procrastination, and all you'll do is think about your idea. Each behavior is vital to Really Rich success. As we know now, it's an integrated system.

The neglect of even one behavior can be your downfall. For all I know, the leadership of Blockbuster was exercising nine out of the ten behaviors, but Blockbuster fell to Netflix because they brushed aside iteration. Sure, Blockbuster leadership might have thought, "The internet isn't all that. Our computerized borrowing system is cutting-edge, and people will continue to come down to our harshly lit stores, in their pajamas, in the middle of the night, to take a movie off the shelf. And if it's not on the shelf because someone else grabbed that video, well, they'll just watch a different movie instead. After all, they've been doing it for years!"

In fact, Blockbuster was so blind to the shifting market that in 2000 the company declined to acquire Netflix for a relatively measly $50 million! This was, in hindsight, the beginning of Blockbuster's end.

Imagine in 2025 opening your Netflix app to find you can't watch a film because a hundred people already have grabbed it—it's a preposterous notion in today's context.

There's a keen difference between getting something so wrong that you have to close the business (as I've done) and refusing to incorporate new information (as Blockbuster did). Really Rich is no guarantee against failure—as we know, you can never fully game the market. But if you happen to get something wrong the first, second, or even third time, you will have become skilled in the behaviors out of which will spring the fourth—and potentially winning—iteration.

What keeps happening, and what will happen even faster over the course of the next five to ten years and beyond, is that more efficient things—meaning, things that provide us with more time, because time is our highest reward, of incalculable value—replace

the more time-demanding things. Streaming a movie via Netflix/
Hulu/HBO/Max/Showtime/Paramount on demand from the comfort of your home is far more efficient than leaving your house to
trudge to a video or DVD rental store. We don't even worry about
such things anymore. VCRs have gone the way of the horse and
buggy.

As a result of time savings, the Netflix innovation alone created
something that's monumentally more valuable than its predecessor.

The same thing is happening right now with AI.

FRICTION IS PART OF ADVANCEMENT

Let's stay within the Blockbuster/Netflix dynamic. At first, there
was friction using this new Netflix tool as people adapted. "How
do I know they're gonna mail me what I ordered? How do I know
it'll be delivered? Plus, I have to be sure I mail it back on time.
Do I really have to give them my credit card? It's twelve dollars a
month—what if I don't watch a movie every month?"

And then time passed.

Netflix got better at what it was doing, and soon enough, you
could order everything online. You could download the film
straight to your laptop, and all of a sudden it's like, "Man, *this is so
much better than it was.*"

In a battle of ideas, the truth will win. And the truth is determined by who does what most efficiently. This kind of time-savings
innovation not only can't be defeated but also has never been
defeated over the course of human history.

Here's another example: Nike used to market four different
types of sneakers—the Jordan, the Waffle, and a couple others.
Today, Nike literally offers thousands of sneaker styles. In part,

this is because Nike figured out how to leverage its website, which operates as a gigantic testing module. As you scroll through hundreds, even thousands of sneakers and click on the ones that interest you, Nike technicians are measuring all these hits. "People are scoping out this particular design? Well, then, let's develop it into a broader product line." The website, with its real-time market feedback, functions as Nike's ideas battleground.

The best companies are the open-minded iteration machines. Reebok didn't choose to iterate in the way Nike has, and for that matter neither did Adidas. As a result, Nike is symbolic, with forward-thinking streetwear and culture, whereas the other two companies are closer to dusty athletic brands. And consider how Nike started: one cofounder, Phil Knight, was at first, in the 1960s, selling Nikes out of the back of his Plymouth Valiant while holding down an accounting job. His partner, Bill Bowerman, formerly Knight's track coach at the University of Oregon, was so obsessed with creating the perfect "waffle" sole that he not only ruined his wife's waffle iron but ended up with severe nerve damage from working with toxic glues and solvents in a small, unventilated space. Nike took a shoe that was sixty years ago considered a specialized item for small communities of runners and brought it to worldwide mass consumption. Today, Knight is worth in excess of $45 billion. How's that for iterative reinvention?

If your business isn't working, it's not because the world is an evil place (though, of course, parts of it are). Thinking like this, or convincing yourself you just have bad "luck," itself an artificial construct, is going to keep you down and pull money straight out of your pocket. The truth is that your business isn't working because *you're doing something wrong.* Not the world. Not the market. You need to tinker with your iteration or adjust one or more of your other behaviors. Either that, or you need more time.

There's a terrific old-timey luncheonette on a corner of Lexington Avenue in Manhattan that was established in 1935 next door to where I used to get my shirts made by a Chinese tailor named Mr. Kent—the luncheonette makes the best egg creams, a New York delicacy, from homespun chocolate. I'd stop in after ordering a few shirts. A hundred years ago there were probably a thousand places like this all over New York City. These days, there's maybe one or two throughout the five boroughs, including this Lexington Candy Shop, as it's called. Now, in 1935, my bet is that the founders struggled at first to keep the business afloat—after all, there were so many competitors. Perhaps they had to iterate their way to better-tasting or more efficiently produced chocolate.

Today, however, the line to get in is often halfway down the block—it's become unusual and chic! It's not that the earlier generation had a bad idea; they had a great idea, and they managed to keep the place running all the way through various wars, economic downturns, and the COVID lockdowns. Instead, its present success is more a reflection that its time had not yet fully matured. Who ever thought chocolate egg creams with tuna melts would become so hip?

Whichever of the ten behaviors needs to be adjusted, when the Really Rich hit a wall, they never blame anyone else. Rather, they tick through their checklist:

- Does my product or service make someone's life easier?
- Am I testing the market to determine what it thinks is valuable?

- Can I tweak the next iteration?
- Is my idea so novel that I simply need more time?
- Am I optimizing for quality of life and not an arbitrary earnings target?
- Do I genuinely rely on kindness in all my interactions?
- Am I humble in my business approach?
- Do I guard against rudeness toward those I work with and for?
- Am I distracted by status?
- Is my futurecasting honest, or does it need to be adjusted?

If something isn't working for you, the answer is—without a doubt—to be found within one of the ten points. And it's up to you to have the guts to put your life to the test.

The Really Rich method is not about dying before society recognizes your value—mad geniuses need not apply: Vincent van Gogh is the furthest thing from our patron saint! This system is instead about getting all that you want within the limits of your lifetime.

CHAPTER 13

Qualities of the Really Rich

COMPLEMENTING THE REALLY RICH SYSTEM, A FEW ADDI-tional actions, if carried out correctly, vastly increase your chances of adding more value to society and unlocking huge financial gain. Your current economic situation is often a reflection of your fundamental behavior and decision-making skills, so daily change starts with the foundations of your beliefs and a mindful attitude toward others. These strategies turn a single- and double-hitter into a home-run slugger. Overlook this chapter at your own peril.

ABANDON STATUS SIGNALING

Attempting to raise your status with material possessions, accents, vocal inflection, name-dropping, vacationing at choice destinations, and the like is social baggage that will distract you from achieving your goals. By concentrating on these outcomes, you lose focus on actually adding value, which is, of course, the sole method of building wealth in the first place.

Beyond being the "wrong road to take" when attempting to live a meaningful and valuable life, status signaling will make you miserable. It's a game with no winner, simply because there will always be someone with more resources than you. You can only accept empty "micro-wins" from getting a one up on someone in your local environment.

And because status is entirely imagined, you're playing a false game. Last time I checked, there's no "American Express Card-holder" gene.

Abandon this kind of signaling as soon as possible and monitor your behavior for when it pops up again (it will). Develop mindfulness around when you're saying something simply to improve how you look to someone else. You'll be shocked how many things you do in your life to climb up a microstep in rank.

In other words, you should strive to build wealth, not refine the skill of appearing wealthy. It's a shortcut that will leave you with very little over the long run.

Comically, those who cling to their status may find your value-creative behavior maddening. You'll be challenged, prodded, and may even face mild forms of abuse. You've escaped the system and live by your own code of ethics, tastes, and preferences. Stepping out of the trap of status makes those still imprisoned feel uncomfortable. You may even lose a few friends in the process, but were these valuable friends after all?

EXTEND YOUR TIME HORIZON

The longer the chunks of time you think in, the richer you will become. Nothing meaningful can be achieved overnight, even with the vast amount of technology at our disposal. The kernel of an idea that creates wealth may flash across your mind during your morning shower, but execution takes time. And sound investing takes time to bear fruit.

Your time horizon may be too short. Simply because true wealth is built over massive changes in society, such as moving from agricultural to industrial processes, labor to computing, human-defined computation to AI—it can take decades. Markets move based on future earnings potential, but your investment won't bear fruit before the change is adopted by the mainstream. You can make money from random market fluctuations, but it's unlikely you'll get rich.

The good news is that the rate of change, as drawn out as it may seem to be at the moment, is contracting significantly from where it was before the Industrial Revolution, let alone during the 1990s internet revolution. New technologies roll out faster today than ever before, and the rate of innovation keeps increasing.

COMPETE WITH SKILL, NOT STATUS

When I joined the workforce, graduating from an elite or Ivy League school was viewed as a one-way ticket to success. However, this rarely played out in the field, much to the chagrin of fancy diploma holders.

Currently, most college admissions decisions are arbitrary guesses at general intelligence. Many brilliant people, for financial reasons, can't pay for their chosen school. The diplomas handed out by top universities are becoming the definition of unearned privilege in the United States. The value of that diploma is dropping while the cost of education continues to rise. Which, of course, is theft on the part of colleges and universities. Or, at the very least, a trillion-dollar bait and switch playing out in the form of staggering student debt.

From my experience in banking, the elitist mentality of "I went to School X, so I must do well at the bank" laughably falls apart for many new hires within the first few months. They quickly realize they're not nearly as smart as they thought they were, or they're unwilling to perform the amount of intense work required of them to succeed. I toughened up quickly during my first six months on the trading floor, but it was a startling experience.

Thought you'd get rich simply because you joined the right "club" with a crest and billion-dollar endowment? Think again: you need to provide value. They didn't teach me that in college, unfortunately, and I had to find out the hard way.

If you're going to compete in a cutthroat industry, do so with how good you are at your job and how hard you're willing to work at learning. Don't rest on where you went to college, where your parents work, where your childhood home is located, or what model car you were gifted for your eighteenth birthday.

DO ONLY WHAT YOU WANT TO DO

There's a popular phrase that I keep in my back pocket: if you don't take the money, they can't tell you what to do. It's founded on the idea that your peace of mind isn't for sale—rich and miserable isn't the goal.

No, you wouldn't rather be "crying in your Ferrari than laughing in your Toyota." And anyway, without liking what you do, it's rare that you'll get the keys to the Ferrari in the first place.

It's no secret that when you're doing something you dislike, you'll underperform as compared to when you're doing something you like. When you like something, you can enter a flow state, where you process information more clearly and lose track of time—solving problems most others miss or are too lazy to fix. You become impossible to compete with.

Remember that every decision to do something is a choice not to do something else. The long grind to get promoted in Big Pharma means that you didn't chase your passion for designing the perfect skincare supplement that you've been tinkering with in your home lab. You took the short-term carrot (a salary) and undervalued a passion that perhaps would have led to a whole damn patch of carrots (a lucrative exit).

Do only what you want to do. And make sure you're always paying attention. Because they'll give you tons of money to do what you don't want to do. I've taken millions to do what I didn't want to do. Over time, you may find yourself veering off course only to end up somewhere you never thought you'd be—old and bitter, a stranger to yourself.

HAVE YOUR OWN OPINION

As you pass through this world, you'll amass a set of beliefs and preferences that, hopefully, are based in wisdom. Far too many people are comfortable parroting the beliefs of the loudest on social media, the trending pop artist, or the most vocal in the room at a cocktail party.

Your own opinion is a model of reality that works for you because of real-world testing. Don't tout "luxury beliefs" (or trendy modes of thinking afforded to the rich at the expense of the poor as coined by author Robert Henderson) because they're considered common knowledge. Such idealistic beliefs shared among the elite don't actually have utility in the real world.

Having your own opinion is similar to defining and maintaining a vision. It's your version of the truth that guides you throughout your day.

DEVELOP A SOLID REPUTATION

A reputation for being reliable, trustworthy, generous, and direct is one of the most important things to cultivate as each additional relationship you build compounds, and a network effect emerges. Those who have built extensive trust with a wide variety of people move through the universe with greater ease and expertise. My skits about befriending everyone, from the butcher to the accounting firm president, are only partly humor—being kind and a straightforward collaborator reduces the friction throughout your day and may get you some preferential treatment. Even being a regular at a coffee shop pays rewards beyond the free cup every now and then. When you're running late to a meeting, you'll find the coffee already made for you, the way you like it, because there's a human on the other side of the transaction who wants to help.

I often check into hotels and find a handwritten note and a basket of snacks in my room. It's a great perk, especially when I show up hungry after a long flight. I don't get these perks because I'm a high roller but because, over time, I've developed a real relationship with the people who work there. I know them by name too. They take a few extra minutes of their time to ensure my stay is memorable, and I take time to thank them in return and talk about their business with my friends and colleagues. It's a cycle of support and respect.

Having a good reputation produces a form of automation that works while you're asleep. You cannot constantly make every single inroad to new businesses and relationships, no matter how good your sales team is, but other people can do it for you, for free and at scale. Right now, as you read this sentence, there's probably someone talking about you. What are they saying? What should you consider changing about the way you deal with people to improve what they're saying?

Most likely, you find yourself telling others about people at the two ends of the spectrum: the jerks and the greats. Be great. Being great is not costless; you need to invest time and resources in relationships, but there is a high multiple paid back over time.

In certain high-risk, trust-based environments, such as venture capital or private equity or diamond dealing, having others vouch for your character means the difference between success and failure. You'll never enter an elite system of dealmaking and collaboration with a poor reputation.

This brings us to the heart of the matter: concrete, nuts-and-bolts strategies for attaining wealth faster and maintaining it with greater ease supplement the principles I've laid out in the previous chapters. Some are obvious; some may seem obscure at first glance.

For the sake of simplicity, I've divided these strategic behaviors into three macro categories: mental behaviors (or mindset), financial behaviors, and human capital.

MENTAL BEHAVIORS
DEFINING A VISION

A future-cast vision is the imagined end state of whatever you're trying to achieve that is so clearly defined it feels real. There are a handful of ways to describe this practice: visualization, starting with the end in mind, manifestation. It's not voodoo—it's the practice of deciding what you want so that you'll know if you're (1) pointed in the right direction on the long trail to achievement; and (2) able to sound the alarm bells when you're not on the right path.

Defining the vision clearly and building an emotional connection to it can produce the effect of belief that some people experience as a physical feeling in the body. Belief is what continues to drive the process home even when you're asleep. If you don't clearly define a vision, it's unlikely that you'll be satisfied with the outcomes you receive, because you didn't choose them.

A future-cast vision takes time to develop and internalize. A study entitled "The Predicting Brain," by Regina Pally, shows how repetition in the form of a thought or visualization can lead to subconscious, therapeutic change.[1] This can be achieved with a daily visualization (generally fifteen minutes), where you walk through specific goal-oriented scenes (like a movie) in your mind. Play the vision back and forth to pick up new clues. The greater the detail and emotional attachment you build, the faster your mind will perceive it as real. This process can be continued for as long as it takes for the vision to take root.

Visualization can also be a helpful decision-making tool. I recommend "vision testing" the various scenarios when you find yourself at a fork in the road. Picture yourself executing on the new plan and living it. Can you keep up with the new workflow? Are you getting the creative freedom you need? Are you finding yourself underwhelmed by the vision and do you need to create a new one? Does this scenario meet the needs of your overall vision? Vision testing can provide an incredible amount of clarity quickly.

A vision for what you want is your best friend when things get tough or lonely. And tough and lonely they will surely be at times.

MAINTAINING YOUR VISION

Sadly, most people never spend the time to develop a vision. If they do, it's even rarer for them to maintain it with the outrageous amount of noise that enters our brains daily. Naysayers, news, current events, and economic cycles all attempt to chip away at our vision over time. Scare us out of our saddles, so to speak. Maintaining a vision is, in part, an act of bravery.

A vision is a belief in a future that has not yet come to fruition. And like all oracles, you may find yourself dealing with ridicule and jealousy. Your investment in a vision is as critical as your investment in a stock or private company you believe in.

However, *vision* isn't another word for stubbornness. If the vision is true, to the best of your knowledge, stay the course. Although the market generally gives instant feedback, it may take some time to evolve toward really big ideas. If the market never responds, it's time for modification.

Plenty laughed at the first iPhone for its lack of a physical keyboard and security protocols compared to the incumbent BlackBerry. Now it's nearly impossible to find a phone without a touch screen. Or to find a BlackBerry anywhere. Steve Jobs had a clarity of vision few will ever be able to achieve.

Maintaining a vision is easier when it's written down and tracked weekly in a journal or spreadsheet.

Here's how you track a vision:

- Describe your overall big-picture vision.
- Define monthly goals that point to the vision.
- Define weekly goals that point to monthly goals.

- Outline your weekly goals on Mondays and review them on Fridays to see how you performed.
- Score yourself from 1 to 10 on how you performed each week.
- Graph the overall score.

It's very hard to see if you're making progress without measurement. But with simple graphing, you'll see if you're trending in the right or wrong direction. I catch myself declining when I'm away from my office too long traveling. My performance data calls me back to work with more authority than any to-do list. Sure, any extra work is a pain in the neck when it comes to building your future, but the five minutes on Monday and Friday may keep you on track closer than any other strategy I've come across.

Without a hard method of tracking, drifting on a vision becomes extremely likely. Even a minor drift can set an achiever back months of time on his or her goals.

EXTENDING YOUR TIME HORIZON FOR SUCCESS

If you want to win big, you'll need a big chunk of time. When you're playing in the big leagues developing something new technologically, a new skill, or a service-based business, it takes months and years to succeed. This isn't because of a lack of capacity to work rapidly; rather, it's the time required for the market to fully adopt what you're doing to its maximum capacity.

The same principle applies to investing. What's priced into the market is already priced in today. You're betting on a change that few see or agree with. This is how you earn outside gains in equity investing. Similarly, those who buy companies trading "cheap to their books," or at a low price to earnings (PE) ratio, are betting against the prevailing belief in the market—that the companies are cheap for no good reason. Value investors like Warren Buffet base their entire investment strategy on this principle and are prepared to wait years, if not decades, to see returns.

Here are some common time horizons I use to measure success:

- *Thirty days:* Micro-testing of a new product or service
- *Six months:* Personal habit evaluation (new exercise regimen, diet, mental health practice, etc.)
- *Two to five years:* Investing in a private company
- *Five to ten or more years:* Equity investing in public companies or building a company from scratch

As you can see, depending on the challenge you're looking to solve, there's quite a bit of time input to smooth out the intraday noise of life and ensure you're seeing actual results.

WILLINGNESS TO FAIL

A willingness to fail is a willingness to learn. The fastest to learn and apply what they've learned wins in any game.

Failure + Reflection = Progress

Those unfamiliar with the way machine learning works may be shocked to know that all the code is doing is trying various solutions over and over without an emotional reaction (computers don't have feelings, of course) until one works. After it has processed large amounts of data, a machine can become more and more accurate at making predictions over time because of the "experience" it gained from trial and error. The difference between a human and a machine is the number of trials made per minute and emotions. Robots don't quit if they don't find the answer straightaway—they keep going tirelessly until they find one.

There's no better way to learn than by trial and error in the field. Intellectual learning, from reading a book or taking a course, is a cheap substitute in comparison to gaining real-life, practical knowledge. In the same way that you can read all there is to know about skiing and still tumble down the mountain on your first attempt, true knowledge is grounded in action.

What is common among people we consider to be visionaries or geniuses isn't an innate capacity for knowledge but rather a history of mass experimentation, persistence, and eventual adaptation. There's a reason why practitioners, rather than academics or, worse, critics, are celebrated by society. Society cares about the doers with field experience because they're the ones who change the world for the better. True learning is a result of quality failure.

WILLINGNESS TO CONSISTENTLY TAKE RISKS

Willingness to fail pushed a bit further becomes the willingness to take risks. Taking risks is extending your skill set beyond the known comfort zone into the unknown surroundings at the perimeter. A willingness to take risks generally involves more creativity than a simple willingness to fail because you're constantly inventing new experiments to run outside your usual field of play. This could be as simple as every day calling a new prospect who is far above your traditional comfort level or asking passersby to try your new product to get one-on-one feedback instead of hiding behind a digital ad campaign.

Risk-taking involves something to lose: capital, reputation, health, and relationships, with the opportunity for outsized, exponential gain.

If you're playing in the "known," you're underestimating your potential.

BIAS TO INVEST NOW

The willingness to invest now is a small variation on both bravery and having a vision. However, this is where the rubber meets the road. When you've learned something new and an opportunity presents itself, you must decisively make the change or the investment. As value changes and erodes over time, the opportunity will not be available to you forever. You'll be rewarded at a multiple for being early, before the rest of the marketplace wakes up to what you've learned.

The willingness to invest now isn't solely about financial investment and strategy. You, as a person, are a work in progress. With a healthy self-review regimen, you're constantly discovering new blind spots and weaknesses. Acting on these learnings is critical to upgrading your entire decision-making process. You need to make the changes now, because applying the learnings has a domino effect across your entire life. Here's a secret that too few realize until late in life: your recognition of and improvements to shortcomings now, such as a commitment to fitness, often end up also improving disparate areas of your life, such as focus at work.

FINANCIAL BEHAVIORS
LEARN HOW TO GROW WEALTH

The Really Rich more commonly use various instruments and structures, not because there is some secret or hidden world available only to those with ample resources but because most of these behaviors are irrelevant for the average person who doesn't understand value, time, or money. In other words, most people don't think of money as a behavior.

There's a reason why another word for money is *currency*—it's an energy that flows throughout our culture. Just as there are various means for creating and exploiting what we more familiarly refer to as energy sources, such as oil, solar, and nuclear, the Really Rich consider how to gather and utilize financial currents.

The average American is in serious credit card debt, not from financing the purchase of an asset like a cash-flowing business or rental property but from increasing their standard of living before earning enough money to afford it. In fact, *debt* in common parlance has evolved into a dirty word simply because it's used the wrong way by most consumers. And it's not entirely their fault: banks market credit cards more aggressively than any other product. Culturally, Americans are indoctrinated into taking on questionable debt early in life with student loans. Using credit cards to fund lifestyle payments seems innocent in comparison.

To more informed individuals, debt becomes a powerful tool when you're using it to purchase assets (generally, things that put money into your pocket over time) as opposed to liabilities (generally, things that take money out of your pocket over time). As long as the rate of income you're earning from the asset you purchased is higher than the interest rate you're paying on the loan (debt), you've opened an opportunity that you couldn't have enjoyed without the existence of debt.

Financial tools should be used to maximize the amount of value you can add to society by investing in value-producing assets—a rental property that you've refinished provides a cozy place for tenants to live, just as the car wash you purchased keeps cars squeaky clean in exchange for an affordable fee.

CASH

Cold, hard cash.

Whereas many individuals love accessing their checking accounts and finding a nice chunk of cash sitting there like a dusty trophy in a curio cabinet, the Really Rich view cash as a hot potato that needs to be immediately tossed to someone else— namely, someone who will pay them a fair return. The miserly, Dickensian Scrooge doesn't exist in modern commerce. Wealthy individuals know that money, in the form of cash, is utterly worthless until it's put into motion: via investment, donation, infrastructure, and so on. Swimming in a money pit, albeit, I'd imagine, momentarily satisfying, is about the sole use of an amassed stack of cash.

Cash, beyond collecting dust, is also eroded by inflation, which even in "good times" is artificially manipulated to advance several percentage points every year. Simply, cash needs to be put to work for it to have any future value. The average person would be shocked to see how little cash wealthy individuals have on hand—most funds are tied up in income-producing assets.

Similarly, any company sitting on mountains of cash is a poorly managed company for not deploying it toward innovation, acquisition, or dividend (cash shared with shareholders).

Cash is hoarded by the rich and abhorred by the Really Rich.

Many are familiar with stories of the richest individuals in society securing loans to pay for basic amenities like rent or a home. Of course, these folks are far from broke. And it's not a traditional loan, which has been used by banks to rack up profits against the middle class, but rather a secured line of credit. The wealthiest have so little cash on hand, because it's tied up in assets, that a loan is the easiest (and cheapest) way to access liquidity. Banks are happy to provide these low-interest loans because they're secured by high-quality collateral, such as common stock or a physical asset.

Cash is also taxed. Without getting too far into the tax advantages of capital gains over earnings, I'll just say a fat paycheck is always taxed at a higher rate than an equity or real estate portfolio. Accepting stock instead of cash upon the sale of an asset would also be taxed at a far lower rate if the stock was held for longer than a year. And, of course, cash spent on a company purchase or investment will lower one's tax bill at the end of the year.

EQUITY

Equity represents an ownership stake in another company.

Common stock floating on a public exchange, such as the New York Stock Exchange, is the most popular form of equity asset held. This is partly because of the development in the 1970s of the 401(k), a replacement for the common pension plan. A 401(k) gives individuals the opportunity to design their own investment portfolios that grow on pretax dollars. Employers could match their employees' contributions to contribute to their retirement assets.

Although the 401(k) empowered individuals to make their own choices around where their retirement cash was parked, it generally "handed over the keys" to people who had no education or interest in portfolio management.

Also, unlike a pension, the value of a 401(k) fluctuates wildly with market cycles. For many, this means that depending on when their retirement date lands, they may find themselves with a lot less than they needed. I founded Revise Annuity to solve this exact problem.

If you're not a diehard investor, the most important thing to note about equity is that you should only consider buying an index fund or an annuity tied to an index. The returns in the stock market over the long run beat a simple savings account (and professional stock pickers for that matter) and require little energy to manage. Most importantly, an annuity entirely removes the risk of market loss. You can learn more about this topic at reviseannuity.com.

The Really Rich, however, may opt to use equity in a different way, namely, to express a view on the marketplace. Unlike traders or "scalpers" looking to make a quick buck with intraday or intraweek price discrepancies, the Really Rich take a decades-long view to see real returns on their investment in common stock. In rare cases, a wealthy individual or fund may buy up so much stock that they have a say in corporate decisions and thus take an active role in making the company more profitable or slashing costs for a boost in the share price.

Equity, like other liquid assets, may be borrowed against or used as collateral on a loan. This means that you could buy stock, take a loan against the value of the stock, and go out and buy another asset, like a house. Often, these asset-backed loans are perpetual with competitively low interest rates. Finally, long-term capital gains are tax-advantaged income in comparison to a paycheck.

DEBT

Debt is an instrument that provides funds to an entity (person, company, financial vehicle) in exchange for the promise to return the funds on an agreed date with associated interest. It's a formal "I owe you."

Debt, unlike equity, doesn't represent ownership in the entity financed. However, in a dissolution of the entity, debtholders are paid before equity holders.

There are typically two forms of debt: secured and unsecured. Secured debt is backed by assets such as real estate or securities— a mortgage is an example of secured debt. Unsecured debt isn't backed by assets, but if the borrower fails to pay back the money loaned, he or she could be sued for the payments and take a credit rating hit. Credit cards are a form of unsecured debt.

Debt is a common banking product for individuals making large purchases. For those who use debt as an investment, it may unlock large sums of cash to purchase more assets that you wouldn't have been able to buy out of pocket or with your own cash reserves.

Like many financial tools, it's a double-edge sword. When used intelligently, debt can allow you to access cash cheaply. However, it's often sold to consumers in a way that only benefits the bank— dangerously high interest rates and low maintenance payments make it tough for many to escape the massive interest payments that accumulate over time.

Rich people run up credit card bills to pay for a vacation they can't afford; the Really Rich use debt to buy cash-flowing assets and they pay down the debt over time, never opting to run up credit card debt with its obscene interest.

INSURANCE AND ANNUITIES

Life insurance protects your family from an early, untimely death; annuities insure those against outliving their assets. In America, it's more common to outlive your nest egg than die before you've had the chance to exhaust it. Annuities like those from my insurance company, Revise Annuity, can insure a portfolio against market losses or convert a large sum of money into a guaranteed income stream. The Really Rich embrace risk they understand and have an edge in, while buying insurance on the risk they don't—often financial insurance. Again, to learn more about annuities in detail, you can visit reviseannuity.com.

HARD ASSETS

Hard assets are just how they sound: tangible assets with a fundamental value. This could be real estate, land, metals, minerals, commodities, and fine art or collectibles. Hard assets are of particular interest to the Really Rich because they are both stores of value and may be tax advantaged. Secured loans are frequently backed by hard assets, so you can take cash out of them and still participate in any price appreciation the assets may enjoy.

Hard assets can also present long-term returns with a more predictable cash flow than financial assets.

On the flip side, hard assets are generally harder to convert to cash quickly (they're illiquid). Think about how easy it is to sell a few shares of stock in comparison to selling an oil field or rare painting. Therefore, investors in hard assets should be in it for the long run.

Rich people own very few hard assets beyond their car and home; Really Rich people own diverse portfolios of land and resources that may provide returns unrelated to stock market shifts.

INTELLECTUAL PROPERTY

Intellectual properties (IPs) are intangible assets in the form of patents, copyrights, trademarks, and trade secrets—stores of human ingenuity. Like all assets, they have an intrinsic value, but it may be complex and speculative to calculate. As there's no public market for trading IP, specialized firms, rather than individuals, are usually the ones transacting in this space.

In the United States, IP protection is strong. In other countries, such as China, IP protection is notoriously weak, and there's big money in unauthorized replication. In a digital world, the protection of these assets is becoming more and more complex, especially between countries with competing interests.

Common forms of intellectual property include patents in the pharmaceutical industry that allow for a monopoly on the manufacture and sale of a particular drug for a specified time. This is where drug companies make their largest returns because they can set the price entirely on their own.

IP may be bought and sold or used as collateral in special situations, and of course it is subject to legal and ownership claims, playing a critical role in developed economies. In addition, IP can be licensed for a defined period, which underscores its flexibility.

TAX EFFICIENCY

At a certain income level, tax efficiency becomes one of the most important strategies for individuals and companies: in the United States, asset holders enjoy tax benefits that those who work for their income do not.

A simple example is the CEO of Coca-Cola versus a Coca-Cola shareholder. The CEO may be paid $5 million for his or her work, and this is taxed at the highest rate as income—37 percent at the time of writing. In contrast, an investor with a large holding in Coca-Cola (assuming he's in the top tax bracket too) will pay only a 20 percent tax on a $5 million dividend payout for his 2.3 million shares (think: Warren Buffett).

Similarly, real estate investors can roll over cash from a property sale into a new property without triggering a tax event, thus allowing returns to compound exponentially.

The bottom line is that reducing your tax burden over time may be the difference between having tens of millions and hundreds of millions of dollars because of compounding interest. The biggest challenge to compounding returns is taxation over time.

Tax law, especially in the United States, is so complicated, often comically so, that only a dedicated professional can untangle the best strategy for you. Professional advice comes with a big price tag for wealthy individuals, but the cost savings are equally high.

Although I won't go deep into the history of why we pay taxes in the first place, although I highly suggest that you research this yourself, it's important to note that taxation isn't and never was considered a form of patriotic duty until recently. Those who complain that the rich pay relatively little taxes misunderstand that tax law is designed to promote investment. Employers are tax advantaged, for example, to encourage them to buy new business equipment, make new hires, and break ground on new projects—all of which stimulates an economy. Government understands that a country is only as strong as its growth trajectory and rewards investment in the future. Indeed, a salary or cash payout is taxed higher than any form of disbursement from a business.

In fact, for most of history taxes were viewed as a necessary evil to fund critical governmental activities. Let's not forget that colonial America fought a revolutionary war against taxes they felt were unjust.

Curiously, the wealthiest individuals in a society collect the fewest benefits of public spending from tax collection: public schooling, public health, public security, and so forth. So, the arguments about paying a "fair share" are rarely substantive.

In other countries, such as Switzerland, this is a well-understood reality. Individuals can "negotiate" with individual Swiss cantons to decide on a fixed tax that's predictable and doesn't increase with income. It's similar to paying rent to live in a building. The Swiss seem to say, here's the basic financial amount we need for you to inhabit one of our towns and cover your "split" of policing, fire and emergency services, and other public benefits. Although it's too late for America to take this path, if you've ever been to Switzerland, you'll understand quickly that the system works just fine.

Really Rich people play by the rules to pay the least tax in their jurisdictions. After all, innovation that benefits all should never be disincentivized.

HEALTH AND HUMAN CAPITAL

Various strategies can further assist you in gaining leverage and opening time for both adding value and leisure time. In a previous business, I devoted countless hours to building a template for "Founder Health"—the physical well-being of a business owner. Essentially, health is the most overlooked quality of a founder, but the one criterion that's also most predictive of success and longevity in the marketplace.

Efficient lifestyle adaptations, such as expertise on hand, proximity to work, and frictionless travel, are also part of what I include under this category of human capital. It's important to understand these concepts early and to employ them the moment you can afford to.

HEALTH

As the saying goes, a healthy man has a thousand wishes, a sick man has one.

Your health is your most important asset and should be heavily invested in through exercise, diet, and rest. Peak performance cannot be achieved without health. Your duty to humankind is to continue offering value, so undermining your health is going against nature.

Everyone will develop a personalized exercise regime, but each should include a mix of resistance and cardio training built into their workweek. There's simply no way around this because we're learning more and more about the anti-aging properties of exercise. It's no surprise that many previously "nerdy" tech CEOs are bulking up with martial arts, outdoor activities, and weightlifting. The impact on their brain chemistry and longevity is invaluable.

If you're cheating your health, you'll never be Really Rich.

PROXIMITY

Proximity to work and play is another way of acknowledging the value of time.

A study performed in 2019 about how much an extra hour of commuting time is "worth" to an employee found that each commuting hour was worth about $30,000 in annual salary. In other words, if an employee's firm was one hour closer to their home, they were willing to take a $30K pay cut. This was a truly incredible piece of data because the world soon moved to remote work during the COVID pandemic. Proximity is a big deal for peak performance, and the closest you can get to work is working from home.

Leverage proximity to save countless dead hours in your week. This may mean living in a more expensive home or apartment to be closer to the workplace. The Really Rich never cut corners when it comes to ease of accessing the workplace. A two-hour-a-day commuter will never be able to compete with the guy who walks across the street. Why do you think founders brag about sleeping at the office?

Elon Musk is said to live in a small, inexpensive home a short walk from SpaceX. This isn't a PR stunt or him as the richest man on earth trying to appear humble. It's that he'd rather live close to his rockets and projects than in a fancy neighborhood in the Hollywood Hills. It saves him time and thus he gains an edge on innovation over his peers at competing space exploration companies, namely, Blue Origin, Sierra Nevada, and Boeing.

Moreover, culture and entertainment should be at arm's reach too. There's a reason why it's more expensive to live in New York City than in Lubbock, Texas. Although technology continues to bring us closer together than ever before, there's no substitute for living in culture and innovation hubs. Intellectual stimulation from culture is just another opportunity to absorb valuable perspectives that feed creative endeavors back at the office.

FRICTIONLESS TRAVEL

The stereotype plastered all over social media of the successful businessperson flying on a private jet sipping champagne is a lie that completely misses the point. Any individual who owns or rents a private jet knows it's not about luxury. It's about time.

Commercial travel is filled with friction, unpredictability, security issues, and buckets of stress. Simply, it's a disaster for those who have every minute leveraged and planned. If you have to travel and you have significant resources, it makes absolutely no sense to fly commercial. Flying commercial is the equivalent of filling up your car with strangers before you go to work or taking the bus instead of another more efficient mode of transportation. Do everything in your power to command your own schedule and buy your way out of communal transportation as an optimization tool, not as a form of elitism.

Most glaringly, social media and pop culture continually get these concepts wrong and frame flying private in the context of flaunting wealth or connections. It's a surface-level view that comes from an immature perspective. For corporate leadership, flying private is a way to maximize a meeting calendar—there would be no other way to meet the demands of global commerce with commercial flight.

Because travel is a tool to preserve existing, or generate more, resources over time, it's by definition an asset and not a liability. Luxuries are liabilities. Frictionless travel is an extremely valuable resource in a global, interconnected world.

Think about it this way. If you can show up to the meeting in person and the next guy can't, who do you think provides more value?

Flying first or business class for long-haul travel provides minor conveniences—sleep and work become much easier in the air—but these pale in comparison to private flights that maximize time savings.

DELEGATION

As previously discussed, outsized success comes from interconnectivity and collaboration. The variety of challenges and quantity of tasks required to produce massive innovation are simply too great for any one person to tackle in isolation. Delegation is the art of selecting the right person for a defined role, handing over the role, and monitoring their performance.

Delegation allows an organization to scale intelligently. It's usually the first step to unlocking personal efficiencies. You should be "buying time" as soon as possible by firing yourself from all the tasks that can be performed by others. By opening more time, you can take the role of the navigator rather than the oarsman. If a role can be defined, it can be delegated. Don't make the mistake of trying to delegate anything that you don't personally understand fully.

True expertise is scarce, thus expensive, so few have access to it. The Really Rich invest heavily in expertise because, despite the cost, it's an overall leverage point to have the very best people handle jobs on your behalf. This is common in areas of legal, accounting, finance, and long-term investing. The Really Rich understand that money paid to experts supports their own valid career objectives.

Conclusion

THE FUTURE IS CREATIVE

IN 1981, A FILM TITLED *QUEST FOR FIRE* WAS RELEASED. THERE WAS no dialogue in the movie, other than grunts, because it depicted clans of Cro-Magnon cavemen and women. It was hard at first to take this story seriously—but after a while, the narrative gripped me, and it has become one of my favorite films.

The story is based on one particular clan who, after an attack from a competing tribe, are forced out of their homes. They take with them a critical small fire, some embers, that they use to start larger ones—the clan does not yet possess the knowledge to start a fire from scratch. While they are wandering in a marsh, their small fire is accidentally extinguished when the fire-bearer slips in the water, and so, to survive, the clan leaders assign three cavemen to procure fire from some other neighboring tribe.

This proves harder than you might imagine because fire, which is critical to everyone's survival, is closely guarded and never shared with strangers. After a series of near-death struggles, the trio finally manages to secure a small flame, but that, too, is lost.

Although the film is noted for how it depicted many human-like emotions in the Cro-Magnon, my favorite part concerns the technological innovation that ultimately saves the clan. Rather than perpetually coaxing a small flame to stay alive so they could use it to start larger fires, the clan ultimately discovers the technique for starting fire independent of a perpetual flame: the three scouts brought a woman from another tribe who taught them how to do so.

This discovery, a leap of creativity brought about by years—or probably centuries—of Cro-Magnon iteration, changed the course of human development. This gives us all something to grunt happily about.

ARTIFICIAL INTELLIGENCE IS OUR FRIEND

Like the advent of fire, current and future AI developments will dramatically alter the course of humanity. For now, however, loud voices, ranging from the pope to the European Union to Sam Altman himself, have issued warnings—and in the case of the EU, enacted legislation—to guard against the presumed potential pitfalls and outright dangers of future AI development. Pope Francis observed that the "unique capacity for moral judgment and ethical decision-making is more than a complex collection of algorithms, and that capacity cannot be reduced to programming a machine."[1] No argument here. I'm not doubting that ethical guardrails need to limit certain AI-related fields, such as destructive weapons systems, but history suggests that the changes from AI we're about to experience over the next several decades will both provide unprecedented benefits to our economy and society and dramatically alter our lifestyles.

With artificial intelligence assuming most, if not all, of society's repetitive and unpleasant jobs, the future will be increasingly creative for humans. In fact, so much of the "doing" will be handled by robotics that the economic hierarchy will begin to flatten as the best ideas arrive from every corner of the world. Unlike well-meaning critics, I see an optimistic and motivational economic future, where anything is possible.

By connecting a robot to the internet, everyone can access the wisdom of humanity in an instant. Whereas a Google search may get you close to a personalized answer, an AI chatbot can deliver the exact response you seek in a tone and format that you find friendly and helpful. AIs will begin to learn your likes and dislikes so they can deliver better information and more entertainment. AI will diminish knowledge imbalances in the same way that Henry Ford's call buttons on his desk allowed him to ring subject-matter experts on staff when he had a contextual question. In court, Ford once responded to claims of being an "ignoramus" by convincing the jury (and his stockholders) that sheer memorization was a dime a dozen, not a proxy for intelligence.

Technology that operates by prompts will unlock the ability to create scalable things cheaply for society, with far less technical skill, which will allow more people from all economic backgrounds to enjoy all the economic rewards. Humanity is on the precipice of taking a giant technological leap that will return to each of us our most precious resource: time.

So, if you're twenty-five years old and at the beginning of your career, what industries should you be thinking twice about? For example, I'm sure we're going to need plumbers, but what about bank tellers? Taxi drivers? Paralegals? X-ray technicians?

This is going to be a wrenching transformation, but not for the entire economy. On the whole, the world is about to get a lot richer and a lot smarter, because information will be available more easily and much more rapidly.

We have to look at AI development like we're students of history. Only fifteen years ago, I had to go down to a temporary lot or to Home Depot to pick out and drag home my Christmas tree. Now I can order it online, and it'll be delivered to my door and set up the next day. Just imagine how much speedier the next fifteen years promises to be.

Yes, there is an acute downside to all this—the change is going to be swift and likely chaotic. A lot of angry people will lose their jobs and will, temporarily, think they have nothing to do. It's not going to be so simple for every bus driver, let's say, to be retrained to maintain robots or to code.

But take the automobile as a case study. The car, for one, has impacted virtually every single industry in the world. You really can say that autos have had something to do with everything, from community development to communications and culture. So, what's so different about AI? AI is on its way to affecting every single thing on the planet, from agriculture to computer science and medicine and more.

The market is in constant flux. Blacksmiths at one time were highly trained, well-earning, skilled professionals, but we don't see too many of them around anymore, except maybe in Colonial Williamsburg. But who wants to live in a museum? Do you really need someone sitting in a corner knitting a sweater for you over the course of two weeks, or would you rather order a machine-made sweater for overnight delivery from Etsy? Not to mention that the economy of colonial America was itself propped up by slavery and indentured servitude. That's not how I would choose to spend my time.

I get that there's nostalgia for the past. Everyone thinks the Roaring Twenties were a hoot, with attractive flappers trashed on prohibited moonshine dancing the Charleston. But there were a whole lot of horrible other things happening in those days, including nasty infectious diseases, the rise of fascism and authoritarian communism, lynchings, and abject poverty. Heck, if you were young and alive in the 1920s, you either just went through a devastating world war or you were about to be drafted into a second one. On second thought, you can take the bathtub gin back.

Still, for many people, the 1920s were boom times—the economy was on fire, at least up to the stock market crash of 1929, and that boom was generated not by government, Big Tech, or Big Science but by individual innovators: Henry Ford's assembly line, Lindbergh's transatlantic flight, Warner Bros.' release of the first "talking" films. This is the trend of our contemporary economy: individuals or small groups end up breaking off from the conglomeration of existing ideas because the streamlined innovator can move faster. In a way, this is the essence of a democratized, antiauthoritarian economy.

THE AGE OF THE INDIVIDUAL HAS ARRIVED

In a democratized economy, of course, the state is aware of what's happening, and a healthy state encourages an open market because, as an organism, so to speak, it wants to live too. An open economy provides a stable, generally peaceful society and a healthy base from which to collect taxes. But in other state models, big corporations lean on the state to weaken it, to stifle, for example, the development of a new product to prevent it from competing with any particular corporation's existing product. This is what's colloquially referred to as the "deep state."

In this instance, the threat isn't coming from the product, per se—for example, the new AI bot—but from the state in cahoots with corporate power. It's not like an artificial intelligence is going to develop itself into a menacing robot that will replicate and prey on us; it's that whoever has control of the machine might program it to do so. It's not the technology we have to fear, it's the application of that technology. And it's not so much the tool but the toolmaker.

Still, it's hard to quash human innovation. Even today, numerous subgroups create open-source AI, quite apart from OpenAI and the one or two most conspicuous and well-funded open-source groups. Innovation and desire will always drive humanity.

One of the terrific insights about ChatGPT is that by making many features free to use, its users are training its models for free. As much as a user benefits from ChatGPT answers, the bot itself is learning and improving with every question it's asked.

Whether or not pressure is applied by a state or corporate power, we're living in a world where individuals are growing more powerful with speedy information at our disposal, which itself affirms the supremacy of being human. You—the individual—grow richer and more powerful through your creative use of artificial intelligence machines. This enables you to extract more value from the market.

But if you think someone in this economy is going to hand you something, think again. If anything, in this burgeoning market, there will be fewer and fewer opportunities to be handed any unearned benefits. Besides, who wants to be handed anything anyway? That lessens your humanity and your self-worth. You have to create value, and this has to spring from your own unique self—and that's why you have no choice but to apply the Really Rich behaviors.

Consider two individuals confronted with hardship. One is given the opportunity to suffer and change and tweak and fight through a stressful environment. The other is given an easy way out before they have an opportunity to succeed. Sure, we'd all like a way out sometimes. Resistance is stressful, and it's scary, but when you're provided a way out before you get to the finish line, you learn nothing. Your growth is prematurely stunted.

The essence of becoming Really Rich is grounded in your ability to iterate until you win. And win you will eventually. The Really Rich person realizes that change and opportunity are everywhere. They understand this world, they deeply respect the responses from the broad market, and they are keen enough to manage the correct ways to behave.

- *I'm going to be kind to everyone because I know opportunity is everywhere.*
- *I know that help can come from unforeseen places.*
- *I know that answers can come from unforeseen places when I need them the most.*
- *And I know my time to create value is limited.*

The Really Rich person is making the best out of the unusual and chaotic atmosphere we find ourselves in 2025, and he or she is fully prepared to navigate the chaos that's sure to follow.

The Really Rich perceive that nothing is predictable. What you *can* do, however, is to get into the habits and rhythms of dealing with uncertainty in an organized and consistent manner. I never know where the answers are going to come from, but I know if I behave a certain way, something is going to work out for me in the long run. My skill set, perhaps like yours, isn't grounded in my education or smarts, to the extent I have any genius at all. No, it's anchored in my ability to approach this unknown world in a consistent and creative way.

I go into each one of my several businesses with the understanding that this is going to be no more than an iteration. If it works, I keep going; if it doesn't work, I try something else. This is how every day looks for me.

I love starting from zero, because starting from zero fills me with the excitement of potential.

The world I'm describing is happening right now, whether you like it or not. Will you navigate it using behaviors designed for the economy that's falling away, or will you adapt to realize a Really Rich advantage?

If you've grabbed hold of the behavior kit I'm offering, you should understand by now that the following standards no longer matter:

- Where you went to college
- What your parents did for a living
- What your high school teacher or college professor said about you
- What your social status is

Instead, double down on the things that make you *you*, and try them out in a variety of different ways. Approach your day in a new way. Treat everyone around you with kindness, and see how many of them will advocate for you when you might need a hand.

What we're talking about here is bigger than the advent of the Internet Age. This is more like the printing press revolution that launched the Renaissance. There's a giant shift underway delivering unprecedented power to the individual.

We can see the first inklings of this in the remarkable performance of ChatGPT. It is already the most powerful computing power ever to be provided to anyone, and each of us can use it simply by asking the "robot" a question. What you don't see are the server farms and billion-dollar data centers chewing through information to provide your answer on a silver platter one or two seconds after you hit Enter. All of this is brought to you by the ingenuity of a lot of smart and dedicated, passionate people.

Who, by the way, are going to make a whole lot of money, as they should, because they're iterating on a product of immense value.

But it's not just them—it's you, too, because all of us relying on AI innovations are provided with the abilities to do our jobs more easily and efficiently.

As far as I'm concerned, the only scary thing about AI is what to do with all the extra time we'll have. Iterations that you've been grinding out for years will be tested so much more effectively. What are you going to do with all those extra work hours? Hopefully, you'll be inspired to create even more value for yourself and others!

The Really Rich model is meant to show how much of a real chance you have now as we move into a new, person-centered age and economy. I'm not particularly trying to inspire you to get off your keister and do this, but I am saying that there's no way to live a Really Rich lifestyle that merges wealth and happiness other than the one set forth in these pages.

The choice is yours: either play the game this way, or find yourself biding your time in a work environment that you know, deep down, is a Faustian bargain.

Look, even the smartest and most iterative people may find themselves, at some point, without a job or perhaps without enough income, but that's okay. Because they will iterate their way into their next job.

Living like the Really Rich takes courage, but it's the courage to bet on yourself.

Take a big bite out of life. Fight through and enjoy the rugged nature of iteration. This is your time to shine.

As we've seen, sometimes—temporarily—the safe option is the best bet. But in the long run, the safe option is actually the most dangerous option. The safe option means you're not using your own brain to be creative and to think on your feet, to think on your own, and to stay flexible by definition.

The safe option means you show up—and not much more. I go to work, I stamp my time card, and then I go home. I watch TV and then I go to bed. I wake up, I go back to work, I stamp my time card, I go home and watch TV...and on and on.

The future will be an environment in which it becomes more risky not to be an entrepreneur than to be one. How many people do you know in their fifties today who suddenly lost their job when their company iterated and downsized? The first to go are often the older, more experienced staff, because they usually cost the most. In a world of shifting technology and innovation, this dynamic will accelerate over the coming decades, which is a shame for those who are laid off because they likely never had any motivation to iterate when they were younger. They may not even recognize who they've become, let alone who they once were, as they wonder how they'll make all those payments on the private schools, the country club, the five-bedroom house on a suburban half acre, and their midlife-crisis car. It's not such a good plan anymore to ensconce yourself in a blue-chip career.

You could have gotten away with this in previous generations because technology didn't drastically change over the course of a lifetime. A friend's father earned a master's degree in computer science in the late 1950s and went on to program and operate those huge IBM computers, the ones with punch cards, in the 1960s; today he can barely figure out how to use an iPhone or a laptop. In the nineteenth century, you could have made horseshoes for ninety years, your entire life, and always had a job, but there may be virtually no skill developed in the 2020s that will be relevant by the turn of the next century.

You had better start iterating today.

THE RISE OF THE TECHNO-GATHERERS

There was a time, long ago, when every day was quite different from the day before. There was a time when you said, "I'm following this food source, this prey, this growth of fruit. And I don't know where it's gonna be tomorrow. So, in the morning, I'm gonna pick up and go over here, and maybe sleep there, and then I'll wake up again, and I'll go to a different here and there, maybe ten miles away." In the hunter-gatherer's life, there was very little in the way of "predictable" or "guaranteed." Our minds were always at work, problem-solving and paying close attention.

Then we discovered agriculture, which was itself a giant iterative change. That's when it became valuable for us to sit on our asses in one place. Not that farming was or is easy, but it's a lot easier and more certain than covering twenty miles a day to track an antelope.

Over centuries, agriculture gave way to monotonous factory work and then the economy adapted to *Dilbert*-style cubicles inside of big corporations—a series of job opportunities over the past several hundred years in which every day looked pretty much the same.

Well, here's a news flash: we're returning to our early days, to what I would call an itinerant, technologically foraging society where yesterday looks nothing like tomorrow.

If we're not exactly hunter-gatherers in the *Quest for Fire* sense, we are in this new economy poised to become what I'd call *techno-gatherers.* Frankly, today I find myself in the same head as some guy with a spear twelve thousand years ago. And that head is: I've got to survive. And it feels a lot better than rubber-stamping envelopes on a conveyor belt.

What are the things I need to do to survive? Maybe start an insurance business to help investors? That looks like a promising source of food. Develop an AI technique that's in demand by the health industry? That'll keep me warm in winter.

Wouldn't you agree that this sort of an economy is closer to our natural state as humans? Aren't we more inclined to hunt and gather, or are we better off sitting in a desk chair, eating processed wheat and sugar and growing ill?

Think about it—the ability to sit on our tailbones at work is thanks to the ingenuity and creativity of those who came before us, who profited off a system in which we're sitting on our asses!

Do we enjoy seeing our heroes in retirement? Daniel Craig's final role as James Bond opened with him playing a shell game on some rum-soaked island. And he's drunk and out of shape, entertaining a gang of hooligans. I sat there thinking: *This is horrible! Bond, get back to your dangerous adventures!* It's not till he's sucked back into the world of espionage that Bond gets to be Bond. Likewise, we absolutely need to be who we are to be happy, struggling in one direction or another to be better, smarter, fitter, or whatever it is you're chasing. The essence of being a human is

- To create
- To solve puzzles and challenges
- To survive

Why would we instead rely on a false promise of corporate safety that weakens us over time? It's like a myth or a mirage. At the very worst, we're like feeder cattle being primed for slaughter when new tech renders our input useless. Only here are we driven to pointless in-fighting.

So, maybe the Really Rich system isn't about the future at all. Maybe it's about returning to our past, to be who we were designed to be: the most bewildering technology to ever emerge from the primordial soup: human beings.

Becoming Really Rich is revolutionary to the extent that it rejects the easy, soft, warm blanket that your parents, your schools, and society at large have offered you as a promise that increasingly can't be kept. It also pushes back on the lie that everyone is out to get you, steal your lunch, and leave you worse off than before. One day you will open your eyes to find that everyone in your path is not holding you back but rather providing a smooth passage, with their chapped hands, ready resources, and unexpected insight. From the dude wiping your windshield at the car wash to the ten-million-per-year CEO who risks losing a limb to join your elevator car—"Going up?"—you better be ready.

The Really Rich behaviors make you rich, not by burdening you with complex skills and strategies but by pulling you closer to who you were meant to be from birth: someone perfectly designed to help everyone around you move forward, faster and faster, in unison, toward something better.

And for offering the best of yourself to those around you, I guarantee that you will be enormously rewarded.

Acknowledgments

As I sat down to write the acknowledgments, I drew a blank.

Not because I don't have anyone to thank, but rather, I'm not sure where to draw the line. Do I thank the barista across the street, Timmy Jimenez (you the man, Tim!), who slips me a free espresso every once in a while, before I thank my own father, Larry, the original Really Rich guy, who feels more at ease joking around with servers and bicycle messengers than his white-collar colleagues? He was the first person who made me believe that anyone *could* be your friend—he lives it. Thanks, Pops.

But perhaps I should back up and give props to the valets (Gio, Oscar, and company) who don't have my car towed when I overextend my welcome in the loading zone? You guys rock.

Certainly to Ned MacPherson for ensuring I learned how to make money on my own so I never had to go get a real job. I am deeply grateful for the accidental mentorship during late nights in Miami. Thanks, brother.

To Michael Miller for saying "I think you'd be oddly *good* at that" when I confided in him on a Chicago summer's day that I'd be making TikToks in my thirties. Your belief helped me believe.

And to Ryan Serhant for being my first high-profile podcast guest who turned into a friend, something like an older brother I never had for two hours straight on our episode filmed in 2023.

Sorry for turning your late arrival into a TikTok (and for giving you zero instructions for how to find the studio).

There's Really Rich behavior emanating from them all.

In fact, there are so many people who make my day better and led to the organization of thought that makes up this book who I don't even know by name.

However, I do know that my brother, Mike, helped—he can joke about anything until it comes to his belief in me. This has been vital to my endurance. Thanks, Mikey Boy.

And that I made my rent in my French Quarter flophouse because Molly Bloom got me a job in that men's clothing store in which I spent several months trying to get back on my feet after leaving Wall Street. I'd be screwed without that act of kindness. I thank you for not laughing at me in one of my lowest moments when many others did.

My business partner, Michael Panik, has appeared to save the day via a serendipitous Instagram DM as the ultimate collaborator. His attitude is always upbeat and ready to tackle the unknown with me as we grow Revise Annuity, day after day. He can think open-mindedly and get the job done too. Textbook example of the Really Rich behaviors. I can't thank you enough.

How did the book come to be, well, on paper in the first place? I know it wouldn't be possible without my agent and coconspirator, Jeff Ourvan, who was confident enough (read: crazy) to take on this project with me. Upon cold emailing agents (that's how I got the ball rolling), many said something to the tune of "This isn't a book yet, but it's a great outline, come back another day." Not great. Jeff simply explained to me that, while it wasn't a book quite yet, he'd be the one to tirelessly work through it with me until it was. Really

Rich indeed. The big "fancy" agencies with celebrities and hip-hop artists lost out on the opportunity to go down the rabbit hole with me on this one before I landed with Jeff and the Jennifer Lyons Literary Agency. This book could have gone a lot of different ways, and Jeff helped bring out the best.

I owe much to my clients at Revise Annuity who have trusted my start-up with their retirement-planning strategy and for allowing me to combine the worlds of tech, finance, and insurance in our own unique recipe. Thank you all, sincerely.

Someone had to buy this lump of text, and no one was more supportive of the message than Dan Ambrosio and his team at Hachette. He calmly allowed me to make all the first-time author blunders without calling me a clown and was accepting of the several hills I had to die on in terms of what would remain in the book. If you thought the intro was a little long, don't blame Dan. More thanks to Seán Moreau and Nzinga Temu for ensuring that the whole package came out looking lovely in print.

Now, in no particular order, a few who have helped me along the way, whether it was a helpful insight, encouragement, or kick in the rear when I needed it: Athanasios Sofronis, Linda DiNorscio, Alexa DiNorscio, Zoe Reback, Stephen Billick, Clay Lemoine, Albert Lachin, Matt Guarino, Dave Fortman, Chase Carlson, Miles Bloom, Oz Kurap, Tim Murphy, Will Dublin, Sourav Goswami, Luis Aguilar, Greg Fields, Zo Agcaoili, Gannon Lavins, Harrison Iuliano, Tom Heffernan, Tom Bilyeu, Chris LiPuma, Alexander Fellows, Mark Jennings, Nicky Cass, Nik Schrobenhauser, Mike Educate, Spencer Slaine, Mark Peters, Joe Tucceri, James Widyn, Hunter Ryan, David Ryan, Jonathan Stein, Charlie Denihan, Hunter Davis, Brandon Galatz, Keenan Reilly, Marc Halpin, Brad

Plotkin, Henry Lopez, whurley, Danny Miranda, Rob Henderson, Ken Nguyen, Scott Clary, Jonathan Tesfaye, Scott Hankins, Johnnie Bernard, Rob Showers, and Neil Solomon—thank you.

And to the friends too many to name and kind strangers in the bar or boardroom, those who've slipped me a coffee or cocktail on the house, facilitated a valuable introduction, gave kudos in the YouTube comment section, sang on the train to Warsaw or Penn Station, who provided me with a little glimpse of how interesting and exciting it is to have the privilege of being alive in a place that rewards good ideas and laughter, thank you.

Notes

Chapter 1: The World Is Not Zero-Sum

1. Dimitrije Curcic, "NBA Salaries Analysis (1991–2022)," RunRepeat, March 25, 2024, https://runrepeat.com/salary-analysis-in-the-nba-1991-2019.

2. Philip Israilevich and Ramamohan Mahidhara, "Chicago's Economy: Twenty Years of Structural Change," *Economic Perspectives* 14, no. 2 (March 1990), https://www.chicagofed.org/publications/economic-perspectives /1990/05marapr1990-part3-israilevich.

Chapter 2: Create Value

1. Joel Rose, "How to Break Free of Our 19th-Century Factory-Model Education System," *The Atlantic*, May 9, 2012, https://www.theatlantic.com /business/archive/2012/05/how-to-break-free-of-our-19th-century-factory-model -education-system/256881/.

2. See, for example, Mark E. Walton and Sebastien Bouret, "What Is the Relationship Between Dopamine and Effort?," *Trends in Neuroscience* 42, no. 2 (February 2019): 79–91.

Chapter 5: Treasure Your Time

1. Dan Kois, "Peter Dinklage Was Smart to Say No," *New York Times Magazine*, March 29, 2012, https://www.nytimes.com/2012/04/01/magazine /peter-dinklage-was-smart-to-say-no.html.

Chapter 6: Reset Your Focus

1. April Witt, "He Won Powerball's $314 Million Jackpot. It Ruined His Life," *Washington Post*, October 23, 2018, https://www.washingtonpost.com /history/2018/10/24/jack-whittaker-powerball-lottery-winners-life-was-ruined -after-m-jackpot/; "Jack Whittaker, Ill-Fated Powerball Winner, Is Dead at 72," *New York Times*, July 1, 2020, https://www.nytimes.com/2020/07/01/us /jack-whittaker-jr-dead.html.

2. Joshua Smith and Chiara Fiorillo, "Tale of Couple Who Won £1.8m on the Lottery and Fell Apart After They Spent Every Penny," *The Mirror*, February 17, 2023, https://www.mirror.co.uk/news/uk-news/tale-couple-who -won-18m-29246416.

3. Chris Joseph, "David Lee Edwards, Powerball Winner, Dies Broke in Hospice," *New Times* (Palm Beach, FL), December 5, 2013, https://www .browardpalmbeach.com/news/david-lee-edwards-powerball-winner-dies -broke-in-hospice-6470093; "$27 Million Powerball Winner Dies Penniless in Ashland at Age 58," *Richmond (VA) Register*, December 3, 2013, https://www.rich mondregister.com/news/local_news/27-million-powerball-winner-dies -penniless-in-ashland-at-age-58/article_320c0a57-0039-568b-8a9e-ca29e19b 2244.html.

4. "48 Workplace Statistics—What Has Changed in 2023? 17. Only 33% of the US and Canadian Workforce Feels Engaged at Work," What to Become, September 12, 2022, https://whattobecome.com/blog/workplace-statistics /#stat17.

Chapter 7: Exude Kindness

1. Sam Mizrahi, "Why Showing Kindness in Business Pays Off," *Forbes*, August 10, 2022, https://www.forbes.com/sites/forbesbusinesscouncil/2022/08/10 /why-showing-kindness-in-business-pays-off.

2. Barbara L. Fredrickson, "The Role of Positive Emotions in Positive Psychology: The Broaden-and-Build Theory of Positive Emotions," *American Psychologist* 56, no. 3 (2001): 218–226, https://doi.org/10.1037/0003-066X.56.3.218.

3. "Secret Santa Millionaire Philanthropist Larry Stewart Dead at 58," Fox News, January 13, 2007, https://www.foxnews.com/story/secret-santa-millionaire -philanthropist-larry-stewart-dead-at-58.

4. Steve Farber, "Kindness Is the New Currency. Are You Cashing In?," *Inc.*, February 1, 2017, https://www.inc.com/steve-farber/this-unexpected -leadership-trait-can-help-your-business-cash-in.html.

5. Yammie Ng, "Brand Marketing Strategy of Blue Bottle Coffee," Medium, August 9, 2021, https://yammiengkl.medium.com/brand-marketing -strategy-of-blue-bottle-coffee-4185e3f07588.

6. "Blue Bottle Coffee Overview," PitchBook, accessed May 20, 2024, https:// pitchbook.com/profiles/company/55436-59#overview.

7. Boshika Gupta, "How Amy's Baking Company Is Doing After Kitchen Nightmares," Mashed, August 18, 2023, https://www.mashed.com/485461 /how-amys-baking-company-is-doing-after-kitchen-nightmares.

8. "'United Breaks Guitars': Did It *Really* Cost the Airline $180 Million?," *HuffPost*, August 24, 2009, https://www.huffpost.com/entry/united-breaks-guitars-did_n_244357.

9. "Ocean Marketing: How to Self-Destruct Your Company with Just a Few Measly Emails," VentureBeat, December 28, 2011, https://venturebeat.com/games/ocean-marketing-how-to-self-destruct-your-company-with-just-a-few-measly-emails/.

Chapter 8: Get Humble

1. Ken Makovsky, "Behind the Southwest Airlines Culture," *Forbes*, November 21, 2013, https://www.forbes.com/sites/kenmakovsky/2013/11/21/behind-the-southwest-airlines-culture/.

2. Makovsky, "Behind the Southwest Airlines Culture," https://www.forbes.com/sites/kenmakovsky/2013/11/21/behind-the-southwest-airlines-culture/.

3. Austin Carr, "Blockbuster CEO Jim Keyes on Competition from Apple, Netflix, Nintendo, and Redbox," *Fast Company*, June 8, 2010, https://www.fastcompany.com/1656502/blockbuster-ceo-jim-keyes-competition-apple-netflix-nintendo-and-redbox.

4. Zachary Crockett, "Shark Tank Deep Dive: A Data Analysis of All 10 Seasons," *The Hustle*, June 30, 2020, https://thehustle.co/shark-tank-data-analysis-10-seasons/.

5. Doric Sam, "'Pat McAfee Show' Moving to ESPN; Contract Reportedly Worth 'More Than Eight Figures,'" Bleacher Report, May 16, 2023, https://bleacherreport.com/articles/10076281-pat-mcafee-show-moving-to-espn-contract-reportedly-worth-more-than-eight-figures.

Chapter 9: Don't Be a Jerk

1. Grace Dean, "Starbucks Workers Say Customers Got Ruder and More Abusive During the Pandemic Because of Clashes over Mask-Wearing, TikTok Drinks, and Product Shortages," *Business Insider*, February 19, 2022, https://www.businessinsider.com/starbucks-baristas-rude-customers-masks-tiktok-product-shortages-throwing-drinks-2022-1.

2. Mary Hanbury, "Rude Shoppers Are Fueling America's Crippling Labor Shortage," *Business Insider*, October 21, 2021, https://www.businessinsider.com/labor-shortage-aggressive-consumers-also-to-blame-retail-restaurants-2021-10?r=US&IR=T.

3. Roger Lowenstein, "Jamie Dimon: America's Least-Hated Banker," *New York Times Magazine*, December 1, 2020, https://www.nytimes.com/2010/12/05/magazine/05Dimon-t.html.

4. Amy Joyce, "Big Bad Boss Tales," *Washington Post*, May 29, 2005, https://www.washingtonpost.com/wp-dyn/content/article/2005/05/28/AR2005052800186.html.

5. Christine Porath and Christine Pearson, "The Price of Incivility," *Harvard Business Review*, January–February 2013, https://hbr.org/2013/01/the-price-of-incivility.

6. Trevor Foulk, Andrew Woolum, and Amir Erez, "Catching Rudeness Is Like Catching a Cold: The Contagion Effects of Low-Intensity Negative Behaviors," *Journal of Applied Psychology* 101, no. 1 (2016): 50–67, https://doi.org/10.1037/apl0000037.

Chapter 10: Ignore Status

1. "Lori Loughlin, US Actress, Jailed over College Admissions Scandal," BBC, August 21, 2020, https://www.bbc.com/news/world-us-canada-53871023.

Chapter 13: Qualities of the Really Rich

1. Regina Pally, "The Predicting Brain: Unconscious Repetition, Conscious Reflection and Therapeutic Change," *International Journal of Psycho-Analysis* 88, pt. 4 (2007): 861–881, https://doi.org/10.1516/b328-8p54-2870-p703.

Conclusion: The Future Is Creative

1. Anthony Faiola and Stefano Pitrelli, "Warning of 'Risk to Our Survival,' Pope Calls for Global Treaty on AI," *Washington Post*, December 14, 2023, https://www.washingtonpost.com/world/2023/12/14/pope-francis-ai-treaty-regulate/.

Index